View
from the Bridge

View
from the Bridge

edited by
Geoff Armstrong

INSTITUTE OF PERSONNEL MANAGEMENT

Typesetting by Photoprint, Torquay
and printed in Great Britain by
Short Run Press, Exeter

British Library Cataloguing in Publication Data

View from the Bridge. – (Developing
Strategies Series)
I. Armstrong, Geoff II. Series
658.3

ISBN 0–85292–541–7

The views expressed in this book are the authors' own, and
may not necessarily reflect those of the IPM.

INSTITUTE OF PERSONNEL MANAGEMENT
IPM House, Camp Road, Wimbledon, London SW19 4UX
Tel: 081-946-9100   Fax: 081-946-2570
Registered office as above. Registered Charity No. 215797
A company limited by guarantee. Registered in England No. 198002

Contents

 **The Contributors**

Geoff Armstrong was appointed Director General of the Institute of Personnel Management in 1992. Before then he was, for three years, the Group Executive Director of Standard Chartered plc, and for four years prior to that he was a member of the board of MB Group plc and a member of the four-man executive group of directors responsible for the overall strategy and operations of the company. Previously he was with British Leyland for seventeen years, most recently as Director of Employee Relations, BL Cars. During that period, he led all of the group-level negotiations with the trade unions at a time of major change in the conduct of industrial relations.

He is a council member of the Advisory, Conciliation and Arbitration Service and a member of the Editorial Advisory Board of the IPM's journal, *Personnel Management*. Until his appointment at the IPM, he was Chairman of the CBI Employment Policy Committee for six years. He has served on various national task forces on training, including the Engineering Industry Training Board for six years; and for two years he was a Government-appointed member of the Interim Advisory Committee on the pay and conditions of teachers.

Eric Caines graduated in Law at Leeds University in 1958, since when he has worked in many parts of the public sector, at home and abroad. After jobs in industrial relations with the National Coal Board and the BBC in the early 1960s, he joined the Civil Service as a direct-entrant Principal in 1966 and has worked in a number of departments. After being involved in two NHS reorganisations in the 1970s and having spent some time working on international pay issues with the World Bank and the IMF in Washington, he has, over the last ten years, been successively Director of Personnel and Finance for the Prison Service with the Home Office, Director of Information Technology in the DHSS and Director of Social Security Operations in the DSS. He then took up a post as Personnel Director for the National Health Service and was a member of the NHS Management Executive.

Mr Caines took up a Chair at Nottingham University in April 1993 to head the Centre for Health Service Management. He is also serving as a member of the Home Secretary's Inquiry into Police Responsibilities and Rewards.

Ward Griffiths was born and educated in Wales. After university, he taught English for four years before joining British Steel where he progressed to senior posts in personnel management. In 1980, he moved into local government as County Personnel Officer for East Sussex County Council; and in 1986 joined Kent County Council in a similar position, later assuming concurrent responsibilities as Deputy Chief Executive. In 1993 he was appointed corporate Resource Director, managing the County Council's central functions – personnel, finance, property and information systems.

He is a Fellow of the Institute of Personnel Management and a Fellow of the Royal Society of Arts. He serves on industrial tribunals and is an adviser to the Association of County Councils. He writes articles for professional magazines and for the local government press. He is an Editorial Board Member of *Human Resource Management Journal*.

Mike Oram is a management consultant specialising in organisational development and human resource strategy, particularly in relation to internationalisation. He is also an executive director of a technology transfer business, with dealings mainly between Japan and Europe. He was formerly, for fifteen years, Director of Personnel and General Affairs for Toshiba (UK). He was instrumental in helping set up Toshiba Corporation's European operations.

As well as being a businessman, he is involved in substantial academic work, and for more than ten years has been a visiting lecturer at London University in strategic human resource management and personnel management in Europe. During 1982 he was seconded from Toshiba to the London School of Economics as an Associate Fellow in Industrial Relations and Personnel Management. He has close associations with Manchester Business School, where he is a visiting lecturer in Comparative Management on the MBA programme. He is a Vice-President elect of the Institute of Personnel Management.

Laurence Jackson is currently working with a number of clients as an independent organisation consultant. He is a Fellow of the IPM, Professional Adviser to the national Flexible Learning Programme and Chairman of the Manchester Industrial Relations Society. He has also written several articles on business strategy, changing organisation culture, and EC legislation.

For ten years, until July 1993, he was Director of Human Resources at Manchester Airport, where he pioneered a competency-based management development programme and initiated many programmes designed to facilitate the transition to a more customer-centred, commercially focused organisation. Productivity improvements include a multi-skilling agreement which enabled the massive second terminal complex to be maintained with no additional resources, and the successful redeployment of over 300 employees following an organisation restructure.

He started his working life as a Marketing Trainee with East Midlands Gas, graduating to manage a busy showroom, and then worked in corporate Strategy and Personnel for the Nottinghamshire and Greater Manchester County Councils.

Janet Rubin is Head of Group Personnel at W H Smith. Prior to that she was Personnel Director of B&Q; and before that she was Head of Personnel and Training for Principles for Women (part of the Burton Group). Her previous personnel and training career was in financial services and food manufacturing.

She is a Fellow of the Institute of Personnel Management and on the IPM panel of experts, and was a member of the Training and Development National Committee of the IPM.

She has a degree in Economics from Nottingham and an MBA from the London Business School. She is on the Advisory Board of the Department of Employment, is a part-time Civil Service Commissioner and is Chair of the LBS Alumni Association.

Kathryn Riley is a human resources consultant specialising in the financial sector. For eight years, until 1992, she worked at County NatWest Group Ltd, most recently as Executive Director, Personnel, in which position she was responsible for the world-wide group personnel service. Before that she was at the Royal Bank of Canada and Morgan Guaranty Trust Company of New York.

She is a Fellow of the Institute of Personnel Management and is a founder member of Women in Banking and a member of the LSE Forum on Human Resources. She is also a member of the industrial tribunals' Employers Panel. She has given a number of lectures and talks on the subject of human resources and has written articles for *Personnel Management*.

Ewart Wooldridge is currently in the general management role of Director of Resources at the South Bank Centre. A large part of his career has been in human resources management in engineering (Engineering Employers' Federation and EITB), printing (Her Majesty's Stationery Office) and the media. From 1980-1987 he was at Granada Group as Head of Personnel for Granada Television, and subsequently Adviser to Granada Group on personnel matters. From 1987-1993 he was at TVS Television as Director of Personnel and General Manager.

He has spoken regularly at IPM Conferences and contributed articles to *Personnel Management* on the subject of the management of change. In 1982 he won the Personnel Management Essay Competition and in 1988 he received the IPM Daily Telegraph Personnel Excellence Award for a major project TVS had undertaken in training and employee relations.He is an external examiner on the University of Portsmouth BA Business Studies degree course.

Stephen Connock is Personnel and Corporate Affairs Director for Eastern Electricity. In this main board appointment for a company of almost £2 billion turnover, he has responsibility for Regulation Services as well as HR and Corporate Affairs. Prior to joining Eastern in 1992, he was General Manager (HR) at Pearl Assurance – a post he held for five years. From 1979 to 1987, he was employed by Philips Electronics as Group IR Manager, and before that as Group Development and Training Manager.

He is the author of three books on HR, and his latest – *HR Vision* – was published by the IPM in 1991 and is now in paperback. He is a Member of the Institute of Personnel Management, and has been a speaker at the IPM Harrogate Conference on no fewer than eight occasions in the last eleven years.

 # Introduction

Geoff Armstrong

Today we are witnessing a revolution in the personnel profession, as in British business as a whole. Effective practitioners have been forced to reconsider or abandon many of the attitudes and approaches they grew up with: the shift from 'resolution of inevitable conflict' to 'active management of change' is real and profound. Much has already been achieved. Many essential changes have been driven through by far-sighted HR and personnel directors, and their line colleagues. And there is every indication that the function will play an ever more important role in organisational life as we move into the next century.

Yet some organisations and some sectors have adapted far more quickly and successfully than others, and almost everyone has found it difficult setting out into unexplored territory without a route map. The Institute of Personnel Management has long been committed to making available clear, practical information about managing people. Although we cannot provide a quick fix, we can demystify a widely scattered and often technical body of knowledge and present it in usable form to practitioners. This book brings together the wisdom and experience of some leading players from almost every sector of the economy, in the hope that others will be able to gain insight from their struggles and successes.

The bad old days

My own early career in the motor industry, and particularly as Employee Relations Director of British Leyland Cars from 1979, vividly illustrates the scale of the recent transformation – and how personnel can spearhead many of the crucial changes.

1

When I started work in 1967, industrial relations and personnel in much of manufacturing industry were driven by a series of assumptions. On the technological side, the key assumption was that economies of scale based on standardisation and product rationalisation were the key determinant of who won and who lost in competitive markets. We were trying to make as many as possible the same as possible, and economies of scale were our God.

In industrial relations and personnel, therefore, we set out to standardise people to fit in with what we saw as a rational model for economic performance. The shape of organisation that went with this was heavily centralised. Most of the important decisions on new products, investment and design were taken at the top and centre of the organisation – and then parcelled out down a multi-level hierarchy. It all seemed highly rational, although the coming together only took place at the topmost level.

We then had the task of getting people to work within these apparently rational structures. Typical methods involved rigid job descriptions and work allocated by means of time-study, work-study and standard-setting. Our goal, although we recognised we could never fully achieve it, was to ensure that every employee was doing precisely what they were instructed to do, for as much as possible of their working time. The intention was to maximise unit production, minimise waste and minimise out-of-balance or off-standard labour effort in order to have an organisation which performed with the steady reliability of a Swiss clock.

The implicit model we had in mind might be summarised as follows:

- The clever people at the top define all the tasks the organisation needs to carry out.
- These tasks are then parcelled out through a hierarchical set of boxes known as 'jobs'.
- Each job is further subdivided into precisely measured

elements, definable by the stopwatch or the rigid job description.

- People are trained, incentivised, monitored to conform (and sometimes punished for failing to conform) with the demands cascaded down from the top.

At the time, we all thought this model right and appropriate, yet some of its implications were disastrous. Notice the assumption that top managers know everything worth knowing, and that those below them need to be persuaded or bullied into doing what they are told. Personnel often assumed, in effect, that people are unavoidable grit in an otherwise well designed and smoothly oiled machine. But once you believe that people get in the way of rational performance and simply cause problems (which then have to be sorted out or blamed on somebody else), you will try and turn them into standardised and mechanised extensions of the machine. You never try and draw on their latent enthusiasm and talents in developing and implementing your plans.

People's dissatisfaction and 'grittiness' were manifested in their decision to go off and organise themselves into trade unions. Personnel management was largely about dealing with collective, institutional representatives and not dealing with employees as people. It was concerned with setting up procedures and agreements by which unavoidable change could be pushed through. Particularly in the UK, where we have a tradition of class-based conflict dating back to the industrial revolution, unions concentrated on resisting change or extracting a price – in terms of more inefficiency, more manning, more restrictive practices, more money. At a time when the Japanese were showing that innovation, rapid change and customisation were the way ahead, continuous bargaining for change was still uppermost in most Western managers' lives.

All this had a number of results. We were slow and ponderous in innovating and we saddled ourselves with uncompetitive cost structures and inflexibilities, so we were never as fast on our feet as our customers increasingly wanted. We also had a simplistic and wrong-headed notion about why people came to work. We wanted workers and we got people. Training was about imposing on them the vocational skills we needed now, never about releasing or developing talent, never about giving them generic skills which would enable them to grow to the limits of their potential.

Trade unions were expected to behave like labour-only subcontractors, simply delivering the labour in accordance with whatever agreements we had made with them. And we chafed when time and again their members demonstrated that wasn't how they saw their role and they weren't going along with any such view. We tried not to distinguish between units of labour and treated far too many of our employees as if they were hands: 'Your job is to turn that screw or move that spanner – we don't want you thinking about other things; we want you to switch your brains off; we don't expect you to contribute beyond your job description or time standard. Indeed, if you do try and get involved in other things, it will be seen as unwelcome interference.' Inevitably, all this produced a reaction. Many of the things we did were seen by our employees as unwelcome intrusions on their humanity, on their nature as people. A fiercely confrontational industrial relations scene was the result.

So where did the personnel function fit in? In many ways, we had a prominent and powerful role. We were often involved in the early stages of new product planning, for example, because everybody knew that the management of change could be the slowest part of the journey from recognising a customer need for a product to putting it on the market. For any major proposal, a crucial question always had to be asked – 'Will the unions wear it?' – and only the personnel people could provide an answer. Indeed, the consequences of getting it wrong were so dire that a lot of practitioners saw their primary function as stopping their managerial colleagues getting into holes by initiating changes that weren't absolutely unavoidable. So the department was in a very powerful position, but often spent most of its time saying 'No'. Managerial colleagues sometimes came to see us almost as representives of the trade unions, as part of the problem rather than the solution.

Another aspect of the function was even more significant. The industrial relations gunfighters were the people who decided whether the factories worked or not on a day-to-day basis. They had a high-prestige role based on fire-fighting, trouble-shooting, and permanent bargaining. I learned very fast myself as one of those industrial relations trouble-shooters. On a purely self-indulgent level, it was great fun – very exciting, very challenging. It was you against the world, so the adrenalin really started pumping! By the words you used or the look on your face, you could have an instant impact, good or bad, on your factory.

But although it was very satisfying, it was clearly no way to run a business that had to satisfy customers day in, day out consistently over the long term. The unions presented a claim or an argument against a planned change, management responded, and bargaining went on until a mutually acceptable (to the parties at the bargaining table) compromise was reached. It was a self-contained world called Industrial Relations, which took very little account of what our customers were prepared to pay, what our competitors were doing, what the organisation could afford to carry as a cost, and what we were doing to our long-term prospects.

By 1979, when I took on the job as Employee Relations Director at BL Cars, both the incoming Conservative government and managers in many industries were arguing that it was high time to put an end to a form of industrial relations which was more like Lewis Carroll's chess game than a constructive partnership. And it was often the IR, personnel and training people, together with some of our line colleagues, who said: 'There has to be a better way, but we must be much more open as managers generally about the business and customer imperatives which underlie our operations. We have to redefine the whole role and the organisational concepts we have all been brought up to accept as sacred cows.' The personnel function was really at the forefront in driving through that change.

The break with the past

Partly because it was in such deep trouble, the motor industry was one of the first to face up to the challenges of the late 1970s. Yet right across manufacturing, and right across the Western world, the Japanese forced us to rethink all our conventional wisdom and old working methods. It was they who pioneered quality initiatives, continuous improvement, supplier partnerships, and delighting the customer with better perceived value, although it took us some time to understand exactly what was going on. We realised, of course, that the Japanese were reducing costs and driving inefficiency out of their organisations, but we didn't grasp just how comprehensively different their approach to innovation and effectiveness was. While we concentrated on cutting costs and driving out waste, they were finding new techniques for bringing about change and implementing it fast. (All this has little to do with 'national character'. In his contribution to this book, Michael Oram draws on his experiences at Toshiba to illuminate the remarkable achievements both of the Japanese at home and of 'British managers acting in the context of Japanese ownership and global business strategies'.)

Eventually we began to fight back. The Thatcher government is always given credit for its hard-line trade union legislation; and industries were being forced to shed labour by the imperatives of competitive survival and success. But I think a bigger part of it was that managers – and particularly some leading personnel and industrial relations directors – were saying: 'This isn't the way to go on. There is a better way and we can develop that better way.' Certainly we were an element in a broader shift in management and government thinking, but the influence of the personnel profession was very significant; there was no sense of being dragged kicking and screaming to the party. In both the intellectual formulation of policy and putting it into practice, we were there.

At BL in 1979, when I took the job of Employee Relations Director, I was strongly encouraged by Michael Edwardes to consult widely and draw up a blueprint of the working practices we needed in our factories. Colleagues were encouraged to be no less radical in looking at manufacturing, design, engineering, marketing, customer satisfaction and lead-times. We were beginning to wake up to the impediments to competitiveness we had saddled ourselves with over many previous decades. Of course we had to drive down crippling costs, but we also had to reverse the attitude of resistance to change so that we could become more flexible and more innovative. In the longer term, we wanted to create *a much more empowered workforce*.

We had to do some very brutal things to get the company into a shape so that it could be managed towards the sort of future that was needed. In doing all those brutal things, I can now see with the wisdom of hindsight, we did not spend enough time thinking about how to equip managers to manage in the new world we wanted to create, how to get them to be customer-driven. We should have spent more time with supervisory and line managers thinking through what more was needed in training and development.

One of our first concerns was to overhaul our system of *working practices*. So we came up with an 85-page document, which we presented to our trade union negotiating team representing over 150,000 employees. It contained detailed and comprehensive proposals for procedural change, for the removal of many of the old rigidities and inflexibilities, and for the creation of *an environment where change was welcomed* as a means to delighting customers. At a stroke, we were seeking to reverse many decades of traditional procedures.

At the national union level, many senior officials recognised and were even quite encouraging of that radical approach. Some thought the motor industry was in such deep trouble that only crisis measures could save it. But while some national leaders were waking up to realities, many trade unionists were not, and we had the Devil's own job persuading our powerful in-house shop stewards' committees, which were frequently communist- or Trotskyist-dominated and saw life in terms of class war. Almost any work in a capitalist system was seen as alienating, almost inimical to the human spirit. Permanent bargaining was almost as good in their eyes as permanent revolution.

Most of our shop stewards and employees were not like that, but in the 1960s and '70s their material standard of living had been raised very well by the process of continuous bargaining; it is always difficult to recognise that at some point the merry-go-round has to stop. So some of them had become knee-jerk militants: when the shop steward blew the whistle and said 'We're all out!' our employees' first question was not 'Why?' but 'Until when?' The whole *I'm Alright, Jack* caricature was not too far from the truth. (Some amusing examples of old-style IR at its worst appear in Ewart Wooldridge's contribution to this book.)

We therefore decided to try and bypass the unions by means of direct *communication with individual employees*, to show that we were not just crying wolf or trying to trick them. So, as well as presenting our 85-page document to the trade union negotiating committees, we had it printed as a newspaper and sent to the homes of every one of our employees. And that was considered very radical, almost like spitting in church, because managers *never* communicated with employees, they communicated with trade unions, who then decided what to communicate to their members. During the '80s, we and many other managements had to learn how to communicate in *Daily Mirror* language. (Those still unconvinced of the necessity of this should ponder the alternatives: in the National Health Service, Professor Eric Caines argues provocatively in these pages that 'Working through the professional bodies and trade unions is often a guaranteed way of *not* bringing staff on board.')

The other priority was *training*. As old demarcation lines

became out-dated and new skills and combinations of skills were needed, we introduced distance and open learning. Initially it was the only rapid, cost-effective way to equip many of the craftspeople and technician/draftsmen with computer skills, and it was becoming increasingly clear that computer-aided design and manufacture were the way ahead. Where people had traditionally used pencil and paper or large drawing boards, and blue-collar craftspeople had not written anything, many thousands of them now needed to be re-equipped and re-skilled to operate in that new world. And we found a useful side-benefit of this heavy investment in their skills was that many of the craft and technical people who were most highly respected in their factories became role models for the types of change needed for success. They no longer saw themselves in 'commodity labour' terms and willingly embraced the new responsibilities and opportunities offered to them.

The lessons for today

I am proud to have been involved in BL's pioneering attempts to embrace change and create a more empowered workforce through training, communications and a more constructive style of employee relations, but we were only taking the first steps in a process of continuous transformation. The question we now need to ask is how far British business, and senior personnel figures in particular, have really travelled down that road.

There is no doubt that managers *have* learned on an emotional and intellectual level, although putting theory into practice is always far more difficult. The dawning is there – that what we are about is creating the capacity within the organisation through people to design, develop and deliver the future we are looking for. There is no longer a belief in top-down prescriptions and detailed descriptions for everything that needs to get done. What we are still lacking are the route maps and textbooks we need for today and tomorrow. One of our key roles at the Institute is to help people acquire the new skills – process skills, team-building skills, diagnostic skills – they will need for the years ahead.

This book offers a wide variety of informed perspectives. Here I would just like to sketch in some of the increased opportunities for personnel and the philosophy we must adopt. I will also examine some of the threats we still face and dangerous assumptions HR professionals are particularly well equipped to challenge. Provided we can make a positive contribution as business partners, *and* help our colleagues avoid some of the disastrous errors of the past, a bright future is assured.

One of the key themes is crisply expressed by Stephen Connock later in this book: 'HR activities must contribute directly and unambiguously to business priorities.' The reason is not hard to find. Michael Oram describes an experiment with a group of post-graduate students where they compiled a comprehensive list of factors, internal and external, which can make a significant impact on organisations. *Every one* had important human resource implications. By being involved from the start in all major decision-making, we can ensure that these are taken fully into account. Yet Kathryn Riley cites a senior manager who said he wanted the function to be more 'proactive' – meaning they should sit down 'to write a new maternity leave policy'! Such useful but secondary tasks suit practitioners who are 'administrators by inclination' rather than business partners. Contributors reveal what such a partnership can mean in practice.

The next crucial point for all organisations is that they must be committed to *continuous improvement*. Beating last year's results is important, but performance targets are ultimately set by:

- customers;
- potential customers; and
- competitors.

Today's customers quite rightly demand:

- quality;
- service;
- instant gratification;
- cost-competitiveness;
- flexibility;
- innovation;
- leading-edge products and designs;
- big-company back-up combined with small-company responsiveness.

It is easy to list the obstacles we face. Markets are increasingly difficult, with unexpected new competitors popping up all the time. Product life-cycles are shorter, exchange rates are more volatile, whole economies are unpredictable, and we are threatened with unhelpful and restrictive legislation by the social engineers of the European Commission.

Yet long-term success can only come from customising our products and services, so the customer gets what the customer wants – even if this means that we have to redesign completely the kind of organisation which just pushes standard products out through standard distribution channels in the hope they might get bought. Good returns only come from satisfying customers' needs, and that in turn requires far more attention to the development of employees as individuals and as team members. I am not referring just to star players or prima donnas, the people capable of occasional brilliance, inspiration or invention, but to *everyone* who works for and with us.

Contributors to this book make clear that there is no single effective style of management, yet many winning organisations have changed dramatically in recent years, so that:

- their structures are now far flatter and less hierarchical;
- power is devolved to smaller, customer-based units;
- aims and purposes are absolutely clear;
- headquarter offices are reduced in size, so that they can

provide strategic direction but do not attempt to take or vet (far less implement) most operational decisions;
- distinctions between line and staff functions have become blurred in management teams made up of people with complementary talents;
- management specialisation has been discouraged, with individuals acquiring a portfolio of 'generalised' skills;
- boards have accepted clear responsibility for creating the vision, allocating resources, developing managerial talent and rigourously monitoring performance against targets and external competitors.

Such organisational changes tend to be accompanied by radically altered approaches to people management:

- *Successful businesses commit time and effort to creating a clear and unambiguous sense of purpose and values throughout the organisation.* Employees have no doubts about what objectives are important and what standards they must attain to achieve them.
- *They emphasise to all employees and at all times the absolute primacy of the customer.* Provided they get that message across, the precise philosophies and vehicles they adopt (Total Quality Management, 'after Japan', 'right first time' or 'zero defects') are of secondary significance.
- *They set stretching targets of competitiveness for the organisation as a whole and clear targets for individual employees,* while encouraging and rewarding initiative and contribution beyond these targets. Performance is appraised continuously with a view both to employee development and to early identification and correction of failure.
- *They invest heavily in training, encourage self-development and ensure that the organisation is constantly learning from customers, suppliers, competitors and from leading players in other countries and industries.*
- *They treat employees as respected contributors to success* (rather than as an unavoidable and costly necessity)

through policies such as flexibility, harmonisation of terms and conditions, 'open-door' communication and enhanced opportunities for internal progression.

- *They recruit for the potential they see as well as for current skills in a constant attempt to raise the overall competence level of the workforce and to make possible a flexible and rapid response to changing circumstances.*
- *They take employee involvement totally seriously*, both through established joint consultation machinery (where unions are recognised) and, more important, through direct involvement.
- *They remove unnecessary barriers and status restrictions and adapt their working patterns to fit the needs of the business and employees* to ensure that people can contribute to their full potential.
- *They develop flexible systems of reward linked to contribution and performance* rather than following the 'going rate' or awarding an automatic inflation-plus annual increase.
- *They take a fundamentally optimistic view of human nature*, believing that most people want to do a good job and commit themselves to the organisation's success, provided they are given the leadership and opportunity to do so.

None of this, of course, is either cheap or easy, but it provides a framework for the more specific discussions in the following chapters. Personnel and HR directors are going to have plenty to keep them busy in the years ahead! Yet along with such far-reaching initiatives in people management and its contribution to wider business planning, the profession has another key role to play. If few real-life companies yet conform to the model of the 'winning organisation' I have just sketched in, it is partly because the ideal is so demanding and partly because British business is still often hampered by a number of doctrines which we must make every effort to stamp out. No personnel practitioner should have much truck with the cult of the accountant, pseudo-scientific decision-making or the headhunters' search for heroes – and they need to start saying so! I now turn to these obstacles we face, and must learn to overcome.

Barriers to change

Many assumptions, both conscious and unconscious, still prevent organisations from realising the vision I have described. Take, for example, *the cult of the numbers and the short-term non-solution*. In the USA, the Stock Exchange judges companies largely on quarterly results. The easiest way for a chairman to raise a cheer at a shareholders' or analysts' meeting is to say 'We've reduced our headcount and costs – we've *cut*', although that cannot possibly be the best way to run a business. Such short-termism, lacking vision and sense of purpose, leads to long-term disaster. We have all got a duty to be efficient, but you can *never* cut your way to success. It must always be part of a process of revitalising, recharging and fighting back, with the object of getting the organisation leaner, fitter and better able to compete, better able to deliver.

During the recession of the 1980s, the finance function, which is essentially a cost-cutting function, was understandably pre-eminent. As we move through the '90s, the personnel function will become much more important as a source of ideas, because businesses have lost the old ability to depend on unique brands, products and technologies. The ready availability of IT means that any of those things can be replicated, copied and overtaken very easily unless the organisation as a whole can successfully renew itself over and over again. The real sustainable capacity resides in the people, so the people people are going to be far more influential.

This has nothing to do with going soft, and everything to do with very hard business arguments. Only by enrolling the willing commitment of our people at all levels can we deliver customised service and value to customers. In the words of

Paul Sabin, Chief Executive of Kent County Council (as quoted by Ward Griffiths in this book), 'Financial resources are finite – people's contribution is infinite.' Those working in the personnel function must learn to make this case, and show how to carry it through in practice.

Another common problem is *the search for heroes*. When a business is doing badly, the first thing we do is fire the chief executive, launch a headhunting exercise to find a replacement, bed that replacement in and buy ourselves two years' relief from the pressure. Some of the heroes found by the search process make wonderful transformational leaders, and some do not, but the basic assumption is that the people within the organisation must be at fault and we need to turn out the old and bring in the new.

But that is often wrong: the people who have been there through bad times, given proper leadership (whether externally or internally introduced), may well be capable of creating the new future. In Anglo-American societies, the temptation to discard, to toss out, to search for a new super-hero, is almost automatic, even though it often proves disastrous and sends all the wrong signals through the whole organisation. Everybody starts keeping their heads down so they cannot be seen as responsible for failure and they stop aspiring to get to the top positions, which in any case are thought to be reserved for outsiders. A deeply demoralised organisation is the result.

This is just one form of the common belief, which all personnel directors should fiercely resist, that *people cannot learn new forms of behaviour*. Again, my own experience in industrial relations is revealing. Many of the most effective change managers were precisely the very up-front gun-slingers, who came to realise, even as they were carrying out their jobs, that the confrontational approach was inadequate. They learned from their experience that there had to be a more comprehensive and rounded way of bringing about effective change. Most of them converted very readily into leaders of the new style of thinking, such as Geoff Keeys at Prudential, John Hougham at Ford (now at ACAS), our own Roger

Farrance at the Electricity Association, Mike Bett at BT and many others. They were once at the heart of the rough and tumble, but now they are thinking most strategically about how to make the long term better.

In the real world, although often outside work, *people learn throughout their lives* and are capable of far more than we normally equip them to do. Yet training in the UK is still far too short-term and narrowly focused. Its role in creating and enhancing organisational capacity through people to compete in new markets and create new opportunities is still misunderstood by many line managers and even many of their personnel and training colleagues. Individuals must ask: 'What do I need to learn to contribute more here, to make myself more valuable here, to build up my portfolio of knowledge and skills so as to make myself more marketable if "here" ceases to exist or to satisfy me?' At an organisational level, the essential issue is maximising the pool of talent for making things happen. The personnel profession has a vital role in putting this across.

The government is also making major efforts in this area but, government being government, there is often too much stress on box-ticking. National Training Targets, NVQs, various job-training schemes for the long-term unemployed are all vitally needed; but they are expressed in terms of numbers, whereas we really need politicians to come out with a vision for the UK as a high-tech, high-value-added economy. We should *not* seek to compete with sweatshop conditions or sweatshop pay, but nor do we seek to featherbed ourselves with levels of pay and conditions we cannot afford to sustain. We want to create the capacity in our people because we have the inherent talent to do it – we are good at creating and designing and facilitating and trouble-shooting.

For the profession itself, IPM's programme of Continuous Professional Development is an innovative and systematic way of causing people to learn. Most managers and directors learn accidentally, by being thrown in at the deep end and given responsibility. But individuals themselves can make the process much more systematic and productive. Organisations cannot take all the responsibility for developing their managers. Keeping log books, recording what lessons have been learned, building up a portfolio of skills and setting learning targets are excellent methods for self-development and for identifying major gaps in knowledge and experience. CPD is a valuable way of achieving that, a framework helping people take responsibility for themselves.

Issues of *accountability* can also create barriers to change. This is often a particular problem in the public sector, where managers (for good historical and constitutional reasons) find it difficult to embrace a truly managerial role. One argument goes that democracy gives counsellors specific objectives, so management is about carrying out the will of the people administratively: balancing the books, putting resources in place so they can deliver politically declared imperatives. The democratic process deliberately leaves fudged and unclear who is accountable.

When I was asked by the Secretary of Employment to join the 'seven wise people' on the school teachers' pay and conditions review panel in 1987–9, I was struck very forcibly by how much head teachers saw themselves as just that – as head *teachers* and not as the managers of the schools. Their role was about deploying teachers, not about setting standards, allocating resources, determining budgets, which one would expect any organisation to have to do. The local authority was seen as either the fairy godmother or the wicked witch, usually the latter.

That exemplifies some of the problems in the public sector. Many highly professional and dedicated managers and public servants are frustrated when they cannot deliver quality results and standards, but we are still very hazy about who is accountable to whom for what, and over what timeframe. Pressure from the two-year electoral cycle often leads to short-term sub-optimal decisions, which makes it hard to get the long-term commitment from people you need to build success in. Several contributors discuss such issues in greater detail in these pages. Professor Eric Caines offers a salutary warning

about the difficulties in the National Health Service; Ward
Griffiths shows how forward-looking councils, even in difficult
times, are becoming far more skilled at 'the management of
disintegration'; while Kathryn Riley argues that the retail
banks, and other employers in the financial-services sector,
also need to combat 'the Born to be a Bureacrat Syndrome',
where 'loyalty [used to] equal career security'.

A final issue concerns *the dangers of quasi-scientific decision-
making*. Obviously HR directors have no God-given right to a
seat on the board and have to earn it on merit. Yet people with
a personnel and training background have a unique contribution to make to any management team, provided they come
as business partners and not as spokesmen for a sectional
interest. They are emphatically not there to speak for the trade
unions or absent employees. When Janet Rubin's former
Managing Director called her the 'shop steward on the board',
he was expressing an attitude which now belongs unequivocally
to the past.

Along with their individual contributions, they can make a
huge difference to the *process*. Decision-making is never clear-
out. Boards of directors often endorse or bless decisions which
have become inevitable or have already been taken lower
down the organisation; decision emerge, there is a lot of
consensus building and opinion tapping. The unitary model has
always been a con, except in very authoritarian organisations.
The Japanese view decisions in the round and take a helicopter
view; it is not so much a question of choosing between the
options as of envisaging what success will look like when we get
there and creating actionable plans to make it happen.

Personnel can introduce a healthy dose of realism into the
process of strategic planning, which is *never* just about
number-crunching. It involves looking at the capacity we have,
ways of enhancing it and making the best use of it. Decisions
which are intellectualised and number-crunched to some
abstract but theoretically optimal conclusion never work out in
practice, because someone down the line soon starts wondering what it actually means! The top management get very

frustrated at the incompetence of the people below them, for failing to translate their grand decisions into action. What would have been far better is listening to those people early on, listening to their views and ideas and contributions – and perhaps making a different decision. Boards of directors, as Kathryn Riley points out later in this book, are often lacking in 'real insight into the only resource in an organisation which can sabotage its plans – the people'. A strong personnel presence in the management team can save their colleagues from many costly blunders.

About this book

Exhortation and academic analysis can never be a substitute for experience. The people best placed to help new or aspiring practitioners are the successful Personnel/HR 'Directors (or their equivalents) who have done so much to regenerate British business. This book brings together the insights of leading players from almost every sector of the economy; each was asked to provide lively and personal pieces which addressed all or most of the following questions:

- What is your underlying personnel philosophy, and how is it expressed in action?
- What were the greatest problems your organisation faced in 1993?
- How did you cope with such problems?
- What was the most difficult decision you had to take?
- What are the keys to effective decision-making?
- What are you looking for now in the people you employ?
- Does personnel have a role in the boardroom?
- What is the role of Personnel in meeting today's key business challenges?
- What are the main issues for the year(s) ahead?

Different writers felt free to answer in many different ways.

General reflections can be found alongside detailed case
studies, styles range from the anecdotal to the 'visionary', and
the personnel managed varies immensely. Ewart Wooldridge
worked at Granada Television as part of the 'award-winning,
world-beating team' which created programmes like *Brideshead Revisited* and *The Jewel in the Crown*. Kathryn Riley
discusses the specific issues of motivating 'the deal junkies' in
the City. Laurence Jackson looks at how comparatively low-
grade staff at Manchester Airport could be empowered, given
'not only the skills but also the freedom and confidence' to
make decisons, often at night or weekends, with major financial consequences. This spectrum of different approaches is a
sign of healthy debate within the profession, yet the book as a
whole offers an eloquent and coherent 'view from the bridge'
in the early 1990s. For anyone working in the field, it is bound
to stimulate thought (and creative disagreement) and to open
up many new perspectives.

The winds of change are perhaps at their fiercest in the
public sector. Professor Eric Caines offers a sobering picture of
personnel's difficulties in 'growing up' in the National Health
Service. Far too often, he suggests, organisational structures
remain 'almost feudal', with the function dominated by procedures and by staff 'telling their organisations what the rules
would not let them do'. The result is 'an immature, undevel-
oped function with little self-respect and held in low esteem by
managers', as revealed by the fact that 'very few Personnel
Directors have been appointed to Trust boards'. Major opportunities have already been lost and it is vital that they are not
lost again.

Ward Griffiths of Kent County Council paints a quite
different picture. For the personnel professionals who spend
time and effort 'bewailing [their] perceptions of lack of
influence and absence from the boardroom', Griffiths provides
an inspiring example in his appointment as '*de facto* deputy to
the Chief Executive, later formally confirmed'. Like the rest of
local government, Kent has recently faced exposure to competitive tendering and numerous legislative changes; since May

1993, after over a century of Conservative control, a 'hung' council has introduced further complexities into decision-making. Griffiths stresses the need for personnel practitioners 'to demonstrate a competence beyond [their] professional base', to stand 'shoulder to shoulder with line management in the drive for high-quality public services' and to adopt 'the most effective management practices to be found in either public or private organisations'.

Michael Oram, formerly of Toshiba, explores the myths and realities of Japanese management and argues that national labels are far less important than effectiveness. We *all* need to learn more about control systems and creative problem solving and to put an end to pointless demarcation disputes. While there is often a good case for devolvement, and for line managers acquiring personnel skills, there are also dangers in the kind of 'all-singing-all-dancing generalist structure', where 'the quality level of management may descend to that learned from booklets purchased at railway, motorway or airline bookstalls'!

Laurence Jackson's in-depth study of recent changes at Manchester Airport points to the need for constant innovation, even in highly successful organisations. Jackson firmly rejects the view that HR input should 'represent an afterthought, reacting to financial models, business development plans and capital programmes'. Instead, personnel's contribution at board level has to be far more central: 'to help develop the company's capacity to think and operate strategically, to identify the composition and nature of the workforce required five and ten years ahead to meet company objectives and devise resourcing programmes to achieve these, and to advise on the important legal or other considerations in relation to planned business developments'. 'Where such matters have only been considered *after* major policy decisions have been taken,' the airport now recognises, 'the outcome has tended to be more problematical, and in many cases more expensive.'

Janet Rubin of W H Smith considers the issues facing even successful retail organisations in recessionary times. While it is essential to become 'leaner and fitter', this can never be an end in itself – companies must keep asking themselves; 'Fitter for *what*?' Personnel teams, Rubin reminds us, 'tend not to have to make too many decisions', although they spend a lot of their time trying to influence others' decision-making. To do this effectively, she suggests, they often need to develop their communication and lobbying skills; it is never enough just to set out a clear, well-argued case and to assume colleagues will be convinced. More generally, the people at the bridge have to keep in constant contact with 'the engine room', if they hope to develop within their organisations 'a truly memorable quality of service and a sustainable competitive advantage'.

Kathryn Riley, formerly of County NatWest, examines the particular issues arising in the financial services sector, where companies have often got into difficulties by ignoring all the research evidence and relying on money as the main motivator. She also eloquently puts the case for HR as 'the guardian of an organisation's core values', which sometimes 'has to challenge the organisation to maintain them'.

Ewart Wooldridge of the South Bank Centre in London also draws on his experiences in television to illuminate the crucial themes of teamworking and change management. Fostering 'an environment in which dedication to innovation thrives and failure is tolerated', so essential to success in the arts and media, is just as important in other sectors of the economy. When major change initiatives are envisaged, divisions within the management team are at least as dangerous as organised union resistance, and insensitivity is invariably disastrous: 'Senior management assumptions about "shoving change through" [often] end up snatching defeat out of the jaws of victory'. Such considerations ensure that proven HR professionals will long remain 'in the driving seat of effective management of change'.

Finally, Stephen Connock of Eastern Electricity analyses the competencies needed in 'newly privatised businesses', where 'the previously public sector culture of stability, of rules and of tenure [has given] way very quickly to cost pressures, IT

changes, raised customer expectations and managing regulatory frameworks'. Even more than other contributors, he
argues in detail for the presence of HR Directors on the main
board and predicts that the organisations of the future will be
lean, affiliated, empowered, ethical and subject to constant
change.

▓ Personnel Paradise – How It Was Lost And How It Might Be Regained in the NHS

Eric Caines

From my academic vantage point in Nottingham, I look out over the NHS and the public sector generally with mixed feelings. The mixture is a compound of a strong emotional attachment to both the idea and the ideal of public service (and, unfortunately, its concomitant that it is better to work for the public than to earn money); a belief in the values which are supposed to underpin it, particularly fairness and openness; deep concern that, in all the areas of which I have experience, the service delivered is not as good as it ought to be; frustration at how ineffective my own contribution seems to have been; and a determination to keep on trying to define and set out the prescription for improvement. In simple terms, we owe the public – despite their not infrequent propensity to make us wonder why we bother – much more than they get in relation to what they pay for it.

In the course of a long career in the public sector (during which I have moved with some regularity between general management and support posts), I find that, in searching for the way to bring about the improvements I should like to see, I have travelled the entire length of the spectrum that links systems and people. I used to believe in systems and procedures as the means of eliminating the people factor. Since people could not be relied upon, if left to their own devices, to act in predictible ways, their behaviour had to be conditioned by tightly prescriptive codes and rules. If you designed fair and logical procedures, you reduced the scope for human error – or so ran the theory. You also gave yourself the best possible defence if things went wrong.

24

So far as the personnel discipline was concerned, this view necessarily led to the incorporation of enormous amounts of detail into procedures. Every eventuality had to be catered for. Every 'what if?' had to be explored and frequent reviews undertaken to ensure that the procedures were giving the desired outcomes. People on both sides – employers and employed – became very skilful at using (or exploiting) the procedures, and the personnel function filled up with staff who were more concerned with the how than the what and who often found themselves telling their own organisations what the rules would not let them do. In the industrial relations area, the result of this approach was that negotiations tended to go on interminably, individual appeals were long drawn out, it became almost impossible to dismiss anybody etc. I exaggerate, of course, but not much. The personnel role was a technocratic one; it was essentially about eliminating risk; it was usually about saying no rather than yes.

The change, when it came, occurred both in me and in the context in which I found myself working as I moved, at two or three year intervals, from job to job. It changed most dramatically, and for obvious contextual reasons, after 1979, though the context complemented the fact that, by this time, I was beginning to fill jobs where I was being forced to look for, and look at, the bottom line and determine by what means I was going to try to improve it. It used to be fashionable to say that there is no bottom line in the public sector; but, if the bottom line is regarded as what you are fundamentally trying to achieve, in the public sector it is quite clearly the balancing act of trying to serve both the recipients of whatever service is being delivered and the taxpayer. In short, it is better service for the client and better value for money for the taxpayer.

This is fairly simple to grasp. What is more difficult, however, is to accept that better service and better value for money are not necessarily opposites and that better service cannot only be obtained through the availability of ever-increasing amounts of money. Indeed, it is only when the need always to seek to get more and better service for less money is grasped that the real nature of public sector management becomes evident.

And it is this realisation which starts to define the nature of the modern personnel function. When the public sector manager starts to wonder how he is going to deliver this particular miracle – of achieving more for less, not just today or tomorrow but each day and every day – he sooner or later concludes that the only real course open to him is to try to work with and through the staff he employs. Essentially, they are all he has.

This career progression left me entirely at the other end of the spectrum, believing that systems and procedures mattered hardly at all and that the real challenge was to find all possible ways of enabling staff to give of their best. It was people who mattered; indeed, they were all that mattered. You could have expertly designed systems and poor staff and you would achieve nothing. You could have poor systems and good staff and the chances were that you would thrive. Of course, the best combination was to have good systems and good staff, but what made systems good was that they supported staff effort rather than constrained it and gave sufficient scope and indeed encouragement for inventiveness, judicious risk-taking and the exercise of initiative.

So here we have the present-day prescription for success, certainly in the large labour-intensive public services. Absolutely essential are line managers who understand that there is a bottom line and are well focused on it; who understand that success in achieving their objectives will only be achieved by making the best possible use of their principal resource – their staff; and who realise that getting the best out of staff will be achieved by creating an environment within which their energies and enterprise can be released. Within such an environment, personnel officers will be regarded as enablers rather than controllers.

Paradise lost

Is the public service anywhere near this? With the best will in the world, I have to say that it is not – which, of course, invites the question: 'Why not?' The reasons are manifold and not all that difficult to identify; they can be found to some degree or other in most public services. But since it is easier to see what is wrong by considering a particular service, I shall focus on the NHS, of which I have had the most recent experience.

The great inhibitor in the running of the NHS is politics. Despite various attempts at separating politics and management, Ministers, largely because of their obsession with Parliamentary accountability, have their fingers deep in the details of everyday NHS life and generally expect to be kept out of political trouble by NHS managers. In simple terms, management risk equals political risk and since political risk is a BAD THING, management risk is therefore to be eschewed. For the personnel officer, this means that, at the very least, procedures must be designed largely to take the heat out of any difficult situation rather than to provide the best management solution to it, and any proposed locally beneficial initiative has to be examined and re-examined from the standpoint of possible national repercussions. This breeds undue caution and leads personnel officers to be more concerned with shielding and sheltering their line managers than with helping them to take new directions.

When the politics factor is combined with the vast degree of centralisation which is the general pattern in the public sector, and certainly within the NHS, the effect at field level is crippling.

Supposedly rooted in fairness and evenhandedness, central pay systems and central personnel policy-making have been features of NHS life since the Service was first launched 45 years ago. At present, there are two central pay systems. There are the Whitley Councils, which set the pay and conditions of service of, essentially, all non-professional staff, and the Review Bodies, which recommend pay levels for professional staff. The Review Bodies were invented as part of a deal designed to persuade doctors and nurses in particular not to take industrial action. Disputes involving professionals always cause Governments immense trouble, since professionals generally find it much easier than manual staff to get the public on their side. Apart from pay, general personnel policies for the NHS have always been set by the Department of Health or, more recently, by the NHS Management Executive which, as it happens, is part of the Department.

Common conditions of service for NHS employees might sound reasonable, but the reality has never reflected the central aspiration that staff doing the same jobs (according to the pay grade definition) in different parts of the country should be paid the same amount. Local labour market circumstances differ, and certain types of staff are much more difficult to recruit in some parts of the country than in others. In addition, managers, not unnaturally, frequently want to vary the content of jobs to fit in with their preferred local working arrangements. Both these factors have led to the adoption of a variety of contrivances designed to enable either centrally determined pay levels to be varied or grade definitions to be altered. Most commonly, a job falling within a particular grade definition has been given a different job title to enable a different rate of pay to be applied. Indeed, circumventing the central systems has, for many years, been a way of life in the NHS, accepted but not publicly acknowledged.

More damagingly, however, the adherence to central pay structures has not allowed managers to use pay to reward good performers and penalise poor performers. The NHS pay scene, despite its evasions and creative local interpreting of the central prescriptions, is distinguished by its flatness and overall greyness and, indeed, when one takes into account the low pay levels which apply in many spheres, its drabness.

Personnel professionals in the NHS have, therefore, never been able to fulfil a fully rounded personnel role. They have simply applied locally the agreements arrived at centrally. Local input to the central negotiating process has been minimal and the advice which has, from time to time, managed to percolate upwards through various attempts at briefing arrangements has usually been totally overridden by political expediency. NHS central pay-setting has not been concerned with using pay to get work done to a high standard but with sharing around equitably the amount of money which the Treasury has been prepared to make available.

Personnel staff, therefore, have had no experience at all – or very little – of designing and implementing pay systems and of using them flexibly and imaginatively with a view to motivating people to give of their best. Their use of the central systems has been policed and variations from central rates and terms have had to be formally applied for. Can any system ever have been better devised to stifle initiative and imagination and to breed frustration?

The tragic result is that the NHS personnel function has never grown up. It is an immature, underdeveloped function with little self-respect and held in low esteem by managers.

So tightly have pay matters been controlled from the centre, that the pay system has also determined to a large extent how work has been done locally. Until recently, there has been little attempt at more imaginative ways of using staff. The norm has been rigid working to grade, a high ratio of professional to non-professional staff, and over-extended management structures based on pay levels. The overall pattern was almost feudal with everyone knowing his or her place and very little variation in the way things were done from one unit to another.

No wonder, therefore, that with the advent of Trusts and the enormous amounts of additional freedom offered to them to opt out of central systems, the personnel function has found it difficult to take the necessary step forward and seize the opportunities presented. The standing in which the function has been held by managers can best be judged by the fact that very few Personnel Directors have been appointed to Trust boards.

The challenge faced by Personnel Directors as the NHS

Working for Patients reforms were put in place in 1991 was formidable, but the opportunities were enormous. Finally the circumstance had arisen which the personnel function had been waiting for, indeed demanding, for years – the chance to emerge as a force to be reckoned with and respected in the NHS, one with a significant contribution to make to local effectiveness and one upon which local managers could rely. It would require a lot of fast growing, some risk-taking and some boldness. It would require a sudden cranking up of the total thinking ability of the function, and a general shift on to the strategic uplands from the tactical lowlands where personnel had been encamped for so long. It offered the chance to acquire much-needed professional pride and, just as exciting, ranges of new skills and approaches. It was, unfortunately, a prospect which only a few brave souls were able to handle.

That they were not *made* to pursue the new course which had been laid down before them was and still is a shame. There is a common belief around Whitehall that change simply happens. And so it does, but unless it is directed and driven it is never the change that anybody wants to happen. Indeed, it is most frequently the change that nobody wants to happen. But rather than, as was possible on a number of occasions, scrapping the central systems and making Personnel Directors and their staff stand on their feet and build new local systems and policies because there was absolutely no alternative, Ministers chose to be cautious and develop a policy of waiting until local developments rendered central systems superfluous. And, of course, they are still waiting and there is still no pressure on the field to move at more than a snail's pace. Sadly, the pay policy imposed earlier in 1993 has almost brought the snail to a halt – and has, moreover, carried to ludicrous lengths the age-old policy of evenhandedness. Everybody gets the same, however well or poorly they perform – the Government says so.

The reason for Ministerial caution in relation to dismantling the central pay systems was and continues to be excessive fear of the professional bodies. And, again, this manifestation of an over-reverential attitude to those representing the professions in the NHS is noted and copied at local level. Dealings, both formal and informal, with professional representatives – as with the NHS trade unions – is, though many will be outraged to read this, a substitute for the effective management of staff. What nobody grasps or seems to want to recognise, probably because it makes life difficult, is that the closer management gets to its staff, the more it understands them, the more it builds systems and devises procedures which demonstrate that staff are valued and motivates them, the less of a gap there is for the professional bodies and trade unions to fill. The attitude which is frequently encountered is that 'We must discuss with the professional bodies/trade unions what we should do' not 'This is what we want to do and we need to find the best way of bringing our staff along with us'. Working through the professional bodies and trade unions is often and absolutely the guaranteed way of not bringing staff on board.

But some habits die hard and many personnel officers know the staff representatives they deal with far better than they know their staff. Doing deals, not exercising leadership, becomes a way of life. It also gives that feeling of exclusivity that comes from creating and promoting 'special' ways of doing things. 'Handling' the professions or the trade unions is promoted as a technique not understood by many and indeed quite beyond most people. This is a cop out, but something which the NHS is light years from abandoning.

Another factor which contributes to the mystique on which the personnel function thrives is that, certainly in the NHS, most people stay in the function for far too long. Not that there is much choice. The number of personnel officers who go on to bigger and better things in the NHS outside the personnel field can be counted on one hand. There is no recognised path into any other specialism and progression into general management is, as of now, almost impossible. What is even more depressing is that, looking around the personnel ranks, not merely can one not identify those who have the capability and are ready to take this step but it is equally hard to spot those with the potential to come through to the top in due course. They would like to do so, of course, but attitudinally even the most senior Personnel Directors seem to accept that it is beyond them. Why should anyone be surprised if everybody else thinks the same way?

The pattern, therefore, is of entry to the function from outside the NHS, which is a good thing, followed by either an over-lengthy stay in the function or departure for some other external job, both of which are relatively bad things. This functional self-containment must end. It must come to be seen, by whatever means and as soon as possible, that passage through the personnel function is as good a preparation for general management as is, for example, time spent in finance work. The function must rid itself of its entirely soft image (simply about people – though it is accepted that not in-frequently people regard themselves as having been harshly treated by their personnel departments) and contrive to get itself seen as a mainstream business function. It needs to play down its specialist role and stop seeking to preserve its mystique, which is not to say that it should not aim to be professional in all it does. But it needs increasingly to think of itself as a people *business* function and not simply as one which is concerned with people. Its aim, in a sense, must be to make itself indistinguishable from general management, or at least to be seen as a co-player in the general management game with a contribution to make which is at least equal in value to that made by any other specialist group.

Quite how the breakthrough to a different and enhanced status is to be made is difficult to see, given the way in which the opportunity to achieve it on the coat-tails of the reforms has been passed up. This is not to say that the chances which could have been taken at a gallop will not eventually be taken at a slower pace, but they will probably take a long time and the environment into which new ideas and new ways of doing things will now have to be introduced is – and is set to continue to be – very different from that which existed two years ago.

The Health Service is always affected not just by its own

politics but by the wider political scene. Given the volatility
which surrounds anything to do with health care when the
general political situation is disturbed, efforts will invariably be
made to take a low-key and cautious approach to health service
developments and changes which, though very necessary in
health terms, might raise the political temperature. This is the
current situation, and it is difficult to see how, all else being
equal, it is going to change in the foreseeable future. One is left
therefore, while trying to calculate how Personnel will move
out of the shadows in the NHS, regretting the missing of a
singular chance and contemplating only slow and, if lucky,
steady advances. Unless . . .

Paradise regained?

Most change usually takes place in times of crisis, and it may
well be that the tight financial situation with which the NHS is
going to have to cope over the coming years will force it into
looking as a priority at how to get more and better service from
the million people it employs. The NHS has not really yet
taken on board the need to drive up productivity. There have
been considerable productivity gains, over the last two years in
particular, but these have not so much been positively achieved
as have been incidental upon the new systems which have been
introduced. The search for a competitive edge within the
internal market was much talked about two years ago, but as
some of the tension has now been taken out of the market by a
resurgence of top-down planning – referred to as 'managing
the market' – the talk is once again turning to general financial
stringency rather than market gains and losses. This has left
those who would have claimed to have been successful in the
market in terms of cost, quality and throughput, wondering
why their success has not resulted in a strengthened position.

If a general tightening of the belt occurs and is sustained, the
importance for those in personnel is obvious. Big productivity

gains are only to be achieved by making better use of that large proportion of the total NHS spend which goes on staffing. Personnel officers must learn to talk the language of productivity and must know how productivity gains can be achieved.

In assuming this forward role, they will need help and support and will particularly want to see that the senior management of the NHS is prepared to back them and their general managers if and when ripples are caused. As part of this, the personnel function itself will need strong and dedicated leadership from the centre with a national director who is prepared to give the Management Executive the messages which he will be encouraging his professional colleagues to deliver locally, and is of sufficient weight to be able to carry the Management Executive with him when times are difficult. Unfortunately, one cannot be hopeful that this will happen. Recent history shows that, despite different approaches by a succession of Personnel Directors, Ministers and senior general managers have never been prepared to give personnel issues the priority they deserve. Indeed, there is a feeling in some senior quarters that, given the degree of decentralisation built into the reform process – in theory at least – there may be no need for a personnel presence at the centre at all. To accept this would be the height of folly. The personnel function in the field needs dedicated leadership from the centre and the provision, not just of centrally organised training and development programmes, but of a sense of direction and purpose. The function must be allowed to grow, but it must also be cajoled into growing and, if all else fails, made to grow.

Conclusion

The conclusion to all this must be that the personnel function in the NHS is at a crossroads. It has missed a golden opportunity to start shaping its own future, in part through its own inability – borne of long dependency on the centre – and in part through the reluctance of the centre to remove the props upon which the function has been accustomed to lean. In the normal course of events, progress would now be slow and painful and the necessary enhancements in status and in management involvement would not be easily achieved. A further spur to progress, however, may result from a tightening of the resource situation and the need to find ways of making scarce resources go further through productivity improvements, which will only be obtained through improved labour utilisation. The personnel function must be prepared for this. It cannot afford to miss the boat a second time.

Facing the Future – Supporting Change at Kent County Council

Ward Griffiths

I shall be anxious to have it said of me that I have brought philosophy out of closets and libraries, schools and colleges, to dwell in clubs and assemblies, at tea-tables and in coffee houses (Joseph Addison 1672–1719).

If matters of philosophy at the turn of the eighteenth century were held within an exclusive domain, management theory in the twentieth century is at least partially open to a charge of also having been somewhat removed from everyday application. Academic and 'scientific' outputs have underpinned the growth of specialisms whilst lacking integration with management practice: a failure to communicate and make connections.

Personnel management, in my view, has been no less prone to the dangers of insularity and navel contemplation than the other management 'professions'. Finding recourse in the safety of techniques, we personnel managers can so easily become entangled in a web of routine functions, constantly bewailing our perceptions of lack of influence and absence from the boardroom. How I wish I could claim £20 a time, not to be too greedy, for each article which appears in the personnel press on that recurrent theme.

In this brief account of my contribution to, and perspective on, the management of change in local government I show how Personnel can and must be at the heart of the business. I describe my philosophy and style in helping chart a course for my organisation. I reflect on how and why my role has widened from Personnel alone. Past experience and current challenges are set against future prospects. Anxieties, problems and dilemmas contrast with successes. Experience of decisions, transitions and new roles for management form a backdrop to a consideration of 'Personnel in the Boardroom'.

Personnel – my approach

Seeking, with all due modesty, to emulate Joseph Addison, I have tried in the jobs I have done in personnel management to make my contribution integral to the management effort and explicitly connected with results. My appointment this year to a post responsible for the strategic management of all Kent County Council's central policy and client-side functions, embracing information systems, finance, property and personnel, has given expression to the need for specialist functions to work together in support of the organisation's goals. Operating separately in 'professional' boxes is more likely to hinder rather than help effective line management of service delivery. We are all general managers now.

How does this approach, this personal philosophy, express itself in practice? Since I was appointed to head Kent County Council's personnel function in 1986, I have participated in a management revolution: one which has enabled my Council to stay ahead of the game as local government has been affected by fast-moving and continuous change; one which has resulted in the Council being judged by its peers in 1993 to be one of England's best-managed local authorities. Throughout this period, personnel has been pivotal, characterised by its full involvement in the process of corporate decision-making. We have focused the organisation's attention on vital human resource issues as a critical part of overall strategy and have sought to pursue progressive policies, beneficial to employer and employee.

The local government context – all change!

Kent County Council's role and its public services are central to the social and commercial life of the local community. It is a big county with a large population, some 1,440 square miles and 1.5 million people. The Council's role is at once strategic and local. It stimulates and co-ordinates the activities of others, thereby conserving resources, and deals with county-wide issues such as the International Rail Link, Channel Tunnel, highways, education, social services and public protection and emergency services. Historically and geographically, Kent is the gateway to mainland Europe and the Council has developed significant links with its cross-channel neighbours.

The county's gross expenditure for 1993/94 totals £1,252m and there is a 31,000-plus full-time equivalent workforce. Given the large number of part-time employees, the actual number on the payroll fluctuates around 45,000 people. There is a wide range of managerial, professional and technical staff, who work within an internal market system. At the centre of the County Council, and in the service departments, a small number of functional staff act on behalf of the organisation in developing policy, specifying and purchasing support services, monitoring and reviewing performance. The vast majority of support staff work in internal provider units meeting specified requirements. From 1994 all these functions will become subject by law to a phased programme of exposure to competitive tendering open to the private sector.

Change is now more rapid, continual and far-reaching than any of my colleagues in the local authority can remember. Our functions, operations, structure and finance are all affected. A potent mix! The main driving force has been central government's seeking to ensure increased efficiency, effectiveness, economy (value for money) and a greater emphasis on improving management performance throughout the public sector. Competition for delivery of local services is complemented by the creation of internal markets; sources of finance have been largely centralised; there has been significant deregulation, and trade union reform. Quality, choice, standards and redress are the new watchwords. The Local Government Commission is reviewing the structure of Shire County and Shire District Councils.

All this change is designed to improve public services. The aims are laudable; their application in practice has had fundamental consequences for Kent County Council. In total these have been difficult to handle, not least because central government departments, each initiating their own change programmes, are not noted for acting corporately to ensure consistency between their separate decisions, or for understanding the impact on councils of the accumulated volume of changes, usually to be implemented within short timescales.

So what has all this meant in practice, and what has been my 'View from the Bridge'?

Recognising the forces affecting public services, Kent County Council has fostered the strategic management of policy and resource allocation processes; and has required the Chief Executive, Paul Sabin, to blend public service principles with an infusion of the most effective management practices to be found in either public or private organisations. There is none of the widespread local government system of the Chief Executive being simply 'primus inter pares' amongst Chief Officers. Our Chief Executive is sharply accountable for results and is on a fixed-term contract. He has nevertheless to combine this with a continued commitment to public service and its essential values.

The Chief Executive and I have agreed from the start that we need effective solutions to 'people issues'. We seek to create a strong sense of partnership and a shared understanding of the new directions in public management.

We spend a great deal of time communicating to large groups of managers the nature of the irreversible shifts taking place in the public sector and the management adjustments that are required to anticipate and respond effectively in the interests of services. I have been very fortunate to work with the backing of a Chief Executive who recognises the critical role of people and personnel issues. His leadership of the organisation has been all the more successful because, to use his own words, 'Financial resources are finite – people's contribution is not'.

To alter long-held beliefs and behaviour there has to be some discomfort at the individual level. Transition is unlikely to be real if life goes on as usual. Structural adjustments have sometimes brought about an effective focus in Kent, redefining departments and senior jobs to meet changing requirements. Searching reviews throw the spotlight on basic departmental operations, costs and results. Unavoidable frictions are, however, eased by complementary initiatives. There is constant attention to communications, and participative cross-boundary workshops help break down professional and service-based barriers. Action-learning sets of managers tackle specific organisational issues. Dead colours are constantly removed, new patterns painted in. Throughout we have been determined to 'get ahead of the game', to combat potential organisational inertia and to embrace change positively. If we are to avoid simply being prey to a torrent of external initiatives and demands, we must constantly anticipate and manage ourselves, rather than simply administer. There is, perhaps, a perception that the public sector has to be forced to accept change. I believe that perception to be generally ill informed. In Kent County Council it has had no place at all.

Management principles

Three crucially important principles of change illuminate the Kent scene. The first is an emphasis on 'Management, not Administration'. The traditional reliance on rules, systems, procedures and conventional hierarchy has been replaced by a focus on performance management, with accountability the single most important attribute. This has helped us simplify and reduce the number of management levels – 'flattening the hierarchy'.

Secondly, being 'Close to the Customer' is a statement of the re-ordering of priorities. As a simple phrase, easily remembered, it has great symbolic significance. Customers and service delivery come first. Centrally based top management acts in support, ensuring effective policy direction and appropriate conditions for the delivery of quality services.

Thirdly, we operate a system of management devolution. This is not just delegation. Responsibility and accountability are found at the lowest level of the management chain. Ownership and responsibility for property, information, money and for people lies with the line management delivering services, not with relatively distant central functions.

Employment policy has a critical influence. My role is to ensure that the personnel function's work complements service objectives, whilst taking every opportunity, despite tough cash limits, to seek improvements which benefit and support the workforce.

Performance management

An underpinning system of performance management is an important part of the overall effort. Performance-related pay is just one part of this scheme, but important for all that. Some 12,000 managerial, technical and professional staff are on PRP, linked through individual action plans into policy priorities, enabling the assessment of their contribution against key corporate targets.

In Kent, performance management sets out to improve organisational performance through a planning system with annual core management targets and departmental business plans. These provide the basis for individual action plans and linkage of performance to pay progression. Monitoring of public attitudes to the Council's services completes the information base.

Positive employee responses have been forthcoming on objective-setting, relative adequacy of pay, job satisfaction and low levels of competitiveness between employees. Excessively short-term goals have been avoided and teamworking prospers. Moreover, the increasing need to specify services for

competitive tendering requires similar processes of target-
setting, performance measurement and monitoring. We therefore have in place the means of addressing such issues.
Individual performance-related pay may no longer be an
essential feature of the system. It helped break the mould,
allowing us to cast new models, and performance management
should now be sufficiently measurement oriented to survive
even without an explicit pay link. The pay-related aspects have
nevertheless been a necessary way of sharpening the focus and
ensuring that every individual was involved.

Local pay

A complementary change, instigated in 1990, was the opting
out of national negotiations for Kent's 12,000 administrative,
professional, technical and clerical staff. The move sent out a
clear signal about the County Council's wish to shape its own
destiny.

The national pay system was out-dated and a significant part
of our budget was being settled elsewhere. Local control of pay
was seen as part of the Council's preferred overall policy.

Ninety-eight per cent of staff volunteered to change to local
contracts, featuring a revised grading system, and annual pay
reviews that are harmonised with individual performance
assessments – they previously took place separately.

Communications

In handling major issues such as these, I am always aware that
it is essential to keep in touch with staff feelings and attitudes.
Thus we have, for example, employed MORI to undertake an
attitude survey of all our employees. Out of this evolved a face-
to-face internal communications programme – 'Making

Connections' – which has been a major success in creating interactive dialogue with our managers on key issues.

In addition to being the title for a corporate newsletter, Making Connections is a modular programme designed for over 1,200 middle managers throughout KCC. The aims are to equip managers with the knowledge they need in order to work confidently in a changing organisation with an uncertain future and also to provide relevant opportunities for self-development through action learning groups. One full programme cycle has been completed. The model remains available for us to use again, or to vary to meet new objectives.

The programme comprises introductory workshops, in which delegates have the opportunity to meet the Chief Executive, ask questions and debate key corporate issues. The groups subsequently meet in 'sets' and work on issues which are important to them in their jobs. They return for a half-day feedback session with senior managers some two or three months later. The results of these groups are then handed over to Senior Managers who, in most cases, have responsibility for the area concerned. This enables the ideas to be incorporated in 'the way KCC does things'.

We are working together to retain the momentum. With the challenges confronting local government, it is imperative that the working relationships between senior and middle management and front-line staff run effectively. In effect, we have created a management-dominated forum which also provides managers with a system of support. While staff are always an organisation's most valuable asset, managers are the critical factor for success because they have the responsibility for ensuring the change is managed successfully.

All general managers now

To be a full partner in the senior management system, it is not enough to be a specialist. In the course of my work for Kent

County Council, I constantly seek to demonstrate a contribution beyond my professional base. For example, I headed a
wide-ranging review of work-related education and training
which showed that we could do better for Kent's students and
employees. Basically, too few students over 16 were staying in
full-time education, and many who did stay were unsuccessful
because their courses were inappropriate to their abilities,
aspirations and job prospects.

Proposals and specific targets came out of the review,
including plans to break down the barriers between academic
and vocational courses and between sixth forms and further
education colleges. Another message was the importance of
everyone working more closely together – schools, colleges,
careers guidance, the Training Enterprise Council, industry
and commerce – to tailor work-related education and training
to what the students want and what the employment market
needs.

It is a strategy that has powerful internal dimensions,
because we are wrestling with how to organise ourselves to
deliver our commitment to the National Education and Training Targets. With increased choice for consumers, continuous
improvement in the quality of design and delivery of public
services is essential; and we need life-long learning amongst
employees to make it happen effectively.

A related activity is my membership of the Mid-Kent
Business Education Partnership Board. Comprising senior
managers from leading Kent employers, we aim to satisfy the
increasing demand for a better-qualified workforce and to
assist employers, educators and young people in achieving
relevant skills and qualifications.

Perhaps in part because I am regularly involved in leading
many corporate contributions I became over time the de facto
deputy to the Chief Executive, later formally confirmed. From
the personnel base of activity I had been able to 'read' the
wider scene and give a clear lead towards key corporate
objectives. But my roots in personnel management have

enabled me to stay sensitive to the 'feel' of the organisation and its problems.

Anxieties and problems

In recent times this 'feel' has caused me to realise that external pressures are creating real anxieties amongst staff. Worry and uncertainty about future prospects is a huge problem. Our new organisational directions are clear – a lean 'commissioning' core and a mixed economy of service and support provision. The imminent extension of compulsory competitive tendering to 'white collar' professional services emphasises the fact that the model 'good employer' public sector tradition, with its implied security and continuity of employment and centrally negotiated pay and conditions, is at odds with 'free market' principles. As the traditional obligation of local government to provide services directly is being challenged, so the continuation of their public sector careers is in question in many of my colleagues' minds.

Further uncertainty has been added by the structure review of English county and district shire authorities, which could mean the abolition of Kent County Council in its present form. Rationalisation and change stemming from the review is likely to result in a reduced workforce. While the absolute change may be relatively small overall, many managers are already expressing real personal concerns.

My major problem now is to develop personnel policies in a way which continues to sustain and add value to key business directions and which also supports and prepares staff for a future in which many feel uncomfortably vulnerable. For many managers there is a requirement to metamorphose from career local government officers to entrepreneurial team-based or individual operators. Others' jobs may come to an end as a result of Local Government Review decisions. The

financial context is ever more difficult. Just how do we
maintain morale and motivation in such circumstances? How
do we prevent the best people from leaving, perhaps to new
Councils that may emerge before Kent County Council is itself
reviewed, or to Authorities not covered by the programme.

Whilst we are not without experience in dealing with such
issues, what is different now is the short time-scales.

Facing the future

Structures and competencies

One key response is the increasingly explicit structuring of the
organisation into the purchaser/provider model. For me this
has meant a major personal change – taking on client-side
responsibilities for corporate information systems, finance,
property and review teams, as well as personnel. I am not
expected to be an expert in all these fields – but I am required
to provide strategic management and direction for these core
resource functions. I am on a steep learning curve. For an
organisation employing 31,000 people, we now have a slim
corporate department of some 120 staff. Fewer than a dozen
colleagues fulfil the policy and client-side roles of the central
personnel function. There are similarly cost-effective resources
for corporate finance, property and information systems. The
majority of staff are in the separate Professional Services
Department embracing the provider units. There is a similar
structure within Service Departments. Thus, whilst Kent
County Council is not itself able to offer secure employment to
all its occupational groups, it can help them secure their future
wider employability through gaining new skills in an appropriate organisational setting.

Our people clearly need new competencies if councils are to
continue providing public services amid increasingly complex
financial and political pressures. The development of staff

skills and knowledge is a key element of the personnel programme.

During the past year, I have been a member of a panel of senior managers, convened by the Local Government Management Board, which has considered what kinds of skills and qualities will be required by local authority management.[1] Reflecting the new organisation in my own Council, we soon decided that priority groups will include, on the one hand, the managers who specify services, purchase them and award contracts for their delivery, and on the other, those who provide services, often making use of professional knowledge and technical expertise.

More direct managerial support to elected members in providing leadership in their communities may also be needed – for example by managers helping create effective local networks, not least with the many quangos of appointed people who run public functions. As councils increasingly buy services from a range of alternative providers, another enhanced managerial responsibility involves monitoring, inspecting and regulating services.

New skills and knowledge are therefore clearly needed, In Kent, our Corporate Training Board, an inter-departmental group of Chief Officers and senior line managers, chaired by myself, is developing five themes as the basis for new competencies: 'Competition'; 'Quality'; 'Communications'; 'The Caring Organisation'; and 'Management Development'.

New opportunities

We are not only helping our current managers but also 'opening up' management to people who are already in our employment at other levels. An example is women's development training. Two-thirds of Kent's workforce are female, but this is not reflected in the management profile. So women working for Kent County Council are able to participate in an open-learning programme. 'Springboard', as it is known, provides accessible and flexible open learning. Line managers provide help with in-house workshops and tutorials. Trained women managers facilitate tutorial groups. This large group of staff is being given the opportunity to make a greater contribution to the organisation as well as experiencing self-development.

Flexibility

Another example of the need for clear corporate leadership on employment policy concerns the relationship of remuneration with the purchaser/provider organisation model. The question is how we can maintain a coherent pay system for professional services staff – lawyers, architects, accountants, planners, information systems officers, personnel officers – when new means of providing services, including compulsory competitive tendering, demand employment packages which help support the development of new business directions.

Our professional staff pay structure, whilst flexible and locally determined, is a unified system glued together by centrally monitored and 'quality assured' job evaluation; and with a single salary structure in which performance influences progress. Now staring us in the face is the need to recognise the interaction and consequences of market forces. Preparing a bid to win a tender for the provision of services against external contractors requires freedom to control unit level costs. With labour intensive services, the main area for cost control is self-evident. The way ahead seems unavoidable – 'set the businesses free'. Yet these provider units are currently part of a single employer setting, with consequential policy and legal constraints.

Supporting transition

For those in provider side units the pressures go beyond pay flexibility. Some want to leave the County Council. If they remain 'in-house', there are legal limits on their scope for trading. So they feel they have one hand tied behind their back. Voluntary privatisation can become attractive, as opposed to risking redundancy if a contract is lost under CCT. Under this option services are transferred from the local authority, with the staff then being able to bid for their previous local authority's business and also trade elsewhere. 'Externalisation' may seem to many of our workforce to offer greater control over their job security and future prospects.

Efforts to help staff in these circumstances include means by which they can consider longer-term solutions, develop in different directions and make lateral career shifts. It is a necessary response to the problems caused by the fragmentation of conventional career structures and systems. The current level of uncertainty damages morale and performance and needs to be minimised. People have to be helped to accept the personal and collective transitions which will be necessary, and to take responsibility for their own futures. The issues are being addressed through a combination of measures. Our 'Job Club' services range from individual career counselling and redeployment/retraining advice to access to labour market networks. Support packages are being developed to help groups of professionals assess the implications and requirements of setting up as an independent business.

Transition – a case study

A good example of the changing employment practices we are managing is the decision of Kent's Social Services Department to transfer nine of its elderly persons' homes out of the public sector.

This move was driven by compelling service pressures. Problems with capital funds were at the root of the problem, with Kent unable to finance the investment necessary to bring all of its residential establishments up to the level necessary to meet new registration standards. Social Services management felt they might have to close some of the homes completely – unacceptable in terms of service responsibilities – and so they proposed a transfer to the private or voluntary sector.

Creation of a 'not for profit' charitable trust facilitated the transfer of nine homes to the voluntary sector. Some 280 staff – around 40 white collar and 240 manual care staff – were employed in these homes. A key employment issue was how to protect staff interests, whilst observing legality and ensuring continuity of service to residents. The chosen route (Section 94, EPCA) was selected because:

- it provided continuity of service for a staff group with extensive KCC service;
- there was no redundancy liability for Kent County Council save for those very few staff not transferring;
- there was choice both for staff (who could elect to stay with Kent) and the new employer the Trust (who could select who would transfer).

In the event, all but a handful of staff transferred. The trade unions were assured about the equivalence of the new employment package and secured their own negotiation and consultation rights with the new employer. Nearly two years on, there have been no disputes and a continued good service for the homes' elderly residents.

Key success factors included ensuring that staffing problems were considered early and prevented rather than cured; starting consultation at the soonest opportunity; and enabling staff to influence the process in general and the personnel issues in particular, so that they 'owned' the outcomes. Throughout the process the personnel function was both a catalyst and a direct source of support to the organisation and to the staff themselves. Again our contribution added value to line management's effort and their service objectives.

Decisions in a political context

The positive management of change is therefore a key requirement, with decisions being taken early rather than later, and
with a determination to be 'ahead of the game' and to
anticipate any uncertainty. Much has been written, in many
volumes, about decision techniques. In local government the
position is complex. Professor John Stewart of the Institute of
Local Government Studies puts it this way:[2]

> Decision-making in the public domain is subject to public
> pressure and governed by politics. In these processes
> collective values are established. It is therefore a process
> which in principle is open. Interests cannot be excluded.
> Pressures cannot be denied. Management in the public
> domain cannot operate in an enclosed world . . .
>
> The criteria for decision-making are subject to debate
> and difference. Management in the public domain has to
> recognise that there are gainers and losers from any
> decision, and in the public domain both gainers and losers
> have voices . . . The public interest is rarely clear.

These realities are now all the more explicit in my job
because in Kent the Council has become 'hung' or 'balanced'.
Since the May 1993 County Council elections, no one party has
overall political control. After a century of continuous political
domination by one party, this change is having many and
varied impacts on processes and decisions about policy choices
and resource allocation.

From a focus on the policies and directions of one political
party, there is now a triple dimension, with new and multiple
systems of briefing, reporting and advising. The Council's
policy priorities are being re-examined; its spending priorities
reviewed; its approach to the Local Government Review
determined. Services and supporting functions are under the
microscope in a tough financial climate. Consequences that
may arise for staff are being carefully analysed, explained and
communicated. The Council's spending is already capped, and
changed priorities can only be achieved by redistribution

within the real-terms total – so one service's growth will be another's reduction.

All three political parties value the Kent County Council staff; but all have to pursue increased cost-effectiveness within ever tighter cash limits whilst protecting the quality of service provision. With the compression of NALGO, NUPE and COHSE into the new union, UNISON, we are also re-examining trade union relationships and systems. So alongside the 'hung' Council's formal decision-making processes there is a need for considerable sensitivity of judgement on personnel policies where decisions are rarely, if ever, clear-cut.

Management qualities

The changed requirements of our 'hung', or 'balanced', Council have already caused managers to rethink their communications and information processes. They have had to learn new procedures and conventions; they are finding their time more pressurised; they have to be even more politically sensitive and aware; and they are realising that decision-making may be slower and unpredictable.

Amongst my own direct colleagues in the central departments there are, therefore, many qualities required as we examine and act on those matters that cut across departmental and committee boundaries. My managers already have essential analytical skills. They will also need to operate strategically, showing understanding of the revised organisation and its changing systems, plus political sensitivity and awareness.

Their qualities will be subject to heavy demands. The continuing programme of change exerts heavy pressures on public spending. Local government will no doubt bear its share of the rigours. Cash limits, already tight, are likely to come under yet more pressure. My colleagues' past professional culture is fast being substituted by a requirement for general management skills.

Personnel in the boardroom

In such circumstances the question 'Does personnel have a role in the boardroom?' is easily answered. In my local authority – large and complex, with tough cash limits, a complex political system and a changing way of life – the personnel contribution is a vital component of the top management team.

With competitive tendering proposed for 25 per cent of the total value of personnel services, the reality is that, whilst there are areas where work can be contracted out, key aspects of what I manage are essential to my authority's corporate strategy. So often, though, the lament of personnel directors is that they are left out in the cold, not part of the inner circle of the organisation. I set out to avoid that fate by winning the confidence of my Chief Executive, the elected members and my colleague Chief Officers.

To achieve my goal I have consistently demonstrated a bias towards identifying solutions rather than problems, using my experience and professional training to help others get results. I have positioned the personnel function shoulder to shoulder with line management in the drive for high-quality public services; and on a personal level I have tried to maintain a consistent honesty and openness in working relationships, alongside discretion and sensitivity to colleagues' problems. This is not to blow a personal trumpet, simply to suggest that in a complex and stressful world, some pretty old-fashioned qualities can still go a long way.

In conclusion

Of course there have been, and will continue to be, mistakes. Some things may have been done too quickly, even allowing for the complexity and the pace of change we are wrestling with. Support systems to complement devolved accountability have not always kept pace with needs. The transfer of power out of the centre has not always been fully synchronised with the development of balancing corporate frameworks. No one gets it all right. Overall, though, the pace of change and pressures both internal and external have been anticipated and dealt with effectively through review, adaptation and continual improvement. In my job I have to help bring about flexible service strategies, capable of speedy adjustment. I have to balance corporate policy and frameworks with unit level freedom to act; to look for increased value for money; and to combine cost-effectiveness with treating people fairly and ensuring their views are taken into account.

And when all is said and done, I remember that local authorities' *raison-d'être* embraces the provision of education, protection, care and development and support services. Such purposes should be no less present in our internal staff policies and programmes. Only if we treat our own employees with care, can we in turn expect them to take proper care of the public services with which they are entrusted.

References

1 LOCAL GOVERNMENT MANAGEMENT BOARD, *Managing Tomorrow*, 1993.
2 LOCAL GOVERNMENT TRAINING BOARD, *Management in the Public Domain*, 1988.

♟ Change Tack! – Japanese Methods in a British Context

Mike Oram

A bridge, as I learned early in my working life navigating ships around the world, is the best vantage point from which to view where you are going, where you have just been and generally to see around. It is also a wonderful place to indulge in contemplative star-gazing. It's the same at the top in industry. From neither can you see what is happening in the engine room or other parts below and you have to rely upon others and technology to inform you what is going on and what is over the horizon. But on the bridge you are accountable for getting the ship to its destination safely, quickly and as economically as possible.

I don't want to take the analogy too far but a ship where everyone works hard, individually and collectively, is invariably one where there is respect and trust: up, down and laterally. People know, understand and accept their discrete areas of responsibility. They recognise implicitly that any weak link is a danger to all. Authority that means something is earned rather than acquired by dint of appointment. These principles seem to hold good for ships of all sizes – and for businesses.

Of course, there are always models of efficiency where intimidation and even fear is the ruler – but usually only until something metaphorically gives, snaps or explodes. Organisations not ruled by intimidatory tactics seem, if other forms of control are in place, to give more added value, certainly in the long run. Unquestionably, they are more agreeable and sometimes even enjoyable places to work.

These precepts have undoubtedly helped shape the underlying philosophy for my career in personnel and more general management. For me, creating the kinds of environment where people want to work hard and harmoniously is a starting point. That's not, I would say, in conflict with the new school of human resource management which tends to be more focused on meeting organisational objectives. Goals change from company to company and from time to time. Fundamentally, people's basic nature doesn't change. In all enterprises everywhere there are the same kinds of human being, albeit with different cultural traits and trained and organisationally honed in different ways.

Flexible concerns

I believe that managers must guard against abusing the opportunities which current political and economic forces offer them. The higher one hauls a pendulum one way, the further it will swing the other, when released. What seems like a good opportunity to respond to market forces should first be examined in the context of the longer term. If 'flexibility' becomes a euphemism for 'exploitation', we are back to an abuse of power.

Of all the issues that were considered when Toshiba was planning its first manufacturing plant in the UK in 1980, that of flexibility was to the fore. The first reference to the subject was in the context of a 'flexible team'. The second was 'flexibility in senior management', where the expectation was that they should work for the company, not just for one department or function. It is a sad comment on our industrial heritage that such an explicit statement was necessary.

Within Toshiba, flexibility has been seen as a facilitator of integration rather than a tool of exploitation. Flexibility of working practices, and of hours and patterns of work, have been the usual order of things. The way to increase monetary reward has been from the start and still is to gain a variety of skills and demonstrate the flexibility of mind to use them when and wherever necessary. In the slack periods in business that have occurred, it has not been unknown for a skilled worker to wield a paintbrush. There is also the case when the directors went into the car park and picked up all the litter (after more conventional attempts to tidy the place had not brought requisite results). This was, I should say, in order to emphasise that they were not beyond doing the job, rather than because they had too much slack in other areas of their responsibility. The car park has, since then, generally been litter free.

When changes in the supply of labour and laws governing industrial relations alter the balance, it is my view that we must guard that the opportunities taken up in creating a new and more competitive order of things for Britain are not taken to extremes. We are, compared to the rest of Europe, more easily able to sack or lay off employees, enforce elastic hours, and reduce pay. The contingencies of survival should not only be applied in the context of tactics. Strategic thinking demands a view to the longer term. British managers have a tendency to be tacticians rather than strategists. The litter of industrial battles that have been won, only to be lost in the context of the greater competitive conflict, is clear from Britain's post-war history. A short-term unsustained advantage is devalued if it can't be or isn't carried forward for longer-term sustained advantage.

Commitment, consultation and control

On a slightly different tack, in market economies employees, as other stakeholders in an enterprise, are interested in the success of that organisation, if for no other reason than its capability to keep on employing them. Organisational objectives need to be clear to everyone. Clarity at one point in time about an organisation's vision, is, however, worth nought if that is not consistently followed through.

The same applies at more down-to-earth levels. Employee

appraisal processes that have no feedback loop quickly lose their credibility and lapse into disuse. Communications processes, to be effective, have to be open and two-way. But there is a need for a further element that has been somewhat lacking in the regular British manager's tool kit: control systems. These are the means by which information is fed back and digested and which essentially incorporate mechanisms that ensure that the systems themselves are maintained. The absence of control systems leads to inconsistency of application. Let me illustrate by asking a question. In the organisations in which you have been employed, how many procedures or so-called policies have you seen introduced which have merely 'faded away' rather than been constructively abandoned? Indeed, at a national level I find it personally challenging to try and identify national initiatives in, for example, the fields of education and vocational training that have stood the test of time and been built upon in an ongoing, evolutionary process.

Since the mid-1970s, I have been working with Japanese-owned companies. If there was one element of Japanese management practice which I could pick upon and which I feel would contribute to the efficiency of British management, I think I would choose the way they adopt appropriate and effective control processes. It is at the core of achieving and maintaining the kind of holistic 'total system' mechanisms that serve them so well. The total system needs its own control systems to maintain the 'totalness' of the effort in the enterprise. The whole system, including all of the sub-systems are then focused on the organisational goals, and the controls help to make sure they stay on course. British industry seems to waste so much on introducing practices which do not stay in place long enough to have a chance of making a contribution and which are then sacrificed in favour of the latest gimmick or unthought-through idea from abroad. It's rather like deciding to do away with children as they show no signs yet of contributing to the economic model.

My personal philosophy and my observations in action have

led me to strive to build and maintain simple organisations with short lines of communication, where information gets passed openly and freely, and where there are control systems to make sure this happens, not sometimes, but every time. In different structures and different businesses, the formulae and the language might be different, but the mission stays similar – and I always have a view to the longer term.

Getting commitment through true involvement and participation pays greater dividends to companies and individuals than any popular panacea such as the current vogue for so-called payment-by-results reward systems. If inappropriately considered, these can turn out to be sources of problems rather than hoped-for solutions. There is nothing intrinsically wrong with performance-related pay. It is just that many of those clamouring for payment by results, as with other such remedies, are so often missing the point. The same has been the case with British quality circles.

One of my Industrial Relations tutors years ago was an East London docker turned academic, who made one point that I have never forgotten. During the mid-1960s, joint consultation was the vogue. 'The mechanisms for joint consultation,' he said, 'only truly work in organisations that don't need them.' That is, I feel, the situation with regard to payment by results. An organisation with the right structure, culture and management systems may well end up with a payment-by-results scheme, probably not labelled that, which will fairly and appropriately reward contribution. Trying to bring about organisational change through payment by results is putting the cart before the horse.

Coping with a problem sometimes means dealing with the issue when it is too late. Problem avoidance strategies are much less glamorous but contribute so much more. Indeed, it is probably the creative problem avoidance strategies and the opportunity of working within them that attracted me to join Toshiba, against the well intentioned advice and expressed concerns of friends, mentors and colleagues. They counselled me against joining such a (then) 'small, insignificant company from the other side of the world.' Yet the hardest personal decision that I think I have ever taken was to leave them 15 years later and return to education as a somewhat mature student in order to gain skills and knowledge for a new business venture.

The hardest organisational decisions in which I have ever participated concerned the disassembly and, ultimately, closure of businesses that for years I had helped build up. Reducing in size is not something that the Japanese are unfamiliar with at home or abroad. Here, with skilful local management, they have managed to keep the matter out of the headlines. The issue returns full circle to involvement and participation. Decisions are so much easier to take when they are arrived at jointly, or at least in an open environment. Could anybody conceive that it would be employees who suggested to management that there should be a downsizing in business operations? If all parties have access to all of the available facts, then why should it be surprising that different parties come to similar conclusions?

I am not a consensus decision maker by instinct but by training and experience. The decisions on how to structure Toshiba's first manufacturing plant in the UK were made through a co-operative and wide-ranging project team which involved amongst others, trade union officials. A 'blank page' approach was adopted. The question, 'What kind of company do you want for the future?', was initially written on each of two blank pages. The answers turned out to be very similar. The process and the resultant practices were nonconformist and pioneering, standing today as a living illustration of the benefits of building good foundations and, indeed, of putting into place adequate control systems. As an illustration of these, more than 10 years afterwards, the basic structures for all communications are still there, much as they were designed, but incorporating developments which have built upon rather than fundamentally changed their nature.

I am an unashamed exponent of a 'contingency approach' to personnel management, in the sense that I consider that an intimate consideration of the context and circumstances of a business's needs together with the widest involvement of all those concerned will be most likely to point to the most suitable course of action. Sharing and participating does not, however, obviate the need for leadership in promoting organisational goals, in developing systems and values, and in adopting a problem-solving approach when problems do, even in the best-regulated situations, inevitably occur. 'Visioning' from the top is a vital ingredient. It is the subsequent processes that hone the capability of the organisation, downwards. Having the vision and something to aim for, and knowing how you are getting on are as essential in industry and commerce as they are to racing drivers, mountaineers or to any process of endeavour. Employees need, however, to feel that everyone is singing from the same song sheet. When the actions of top management seem inconsistent with the theme of the corporate song, credibility disappears and the visioning process comes to nought – or, worse, the organisation becomes divided.

Label-free management

Reading many of the books, articles and so forth published during the last decade, one might believe that the only form of management worth having in Britain emanates from Japan. Earlier, North American and Scandinavian management methods were under the spotlight. If there is nothing else that happens during the 1990s, I truly hope that this will become the decade of management processes free of national labels. These are often based upon false premises and can be otherwise quite misleading. My own experience is clearly with the 'Japanese Miracle' in which British businesses under Japanese ownership have bloomed in formerly unheard of ways. Television and automotive manufacturing are notable examples. But, if one looks in sufficient detail, one often finds that the processes being labelled as particularly 'Japanese' have their sources much closer to home. It is often British managers acting in the context of Japanese ownership and global business strategies that have helped to bring about some of the radical and sometimes novel processes that have 'Japanese' labels. In reality, it is the owners who have sought from indigenous managers local adaptations and delivery systems that support the achievement of their business goals.

Some Japanese manufacturing companies are, in some ways, arguably more successful in Britain than in Japan. Towards the end of the 1980s, a worldwide survey of metal-working industries showed that Japanese workers were less satisfied with their lot than workers in any of the other developed nations. (It didn't say they were less committed in practical terms.) Yet even though British workers seemed to be more contented, an earlier study in Britain by the Policy Studies Institute[1] suggested a greater degree of satisfaction on the part of British workers in Japanese-owned companies than in British or other foreign-owned companies.

The quality of workers' satisfaction is not in itself an industrial output. Only the product can provide the measure of a company, whether that product is material or a service. Nissan's British operation is, as measured inside Nissan, arguably more successful than their plants back at home. The uncorroborated views of individuals, maybe – but that such opinions have even been expressed is noteworthy.

Unquestionably, investment capital, its availability and application comes into the frame, but Japanese investments, even in Britain, have usually been linked to long-term investment in human capital. Long-term investments can also have short-term benefits, but rarely the other way round. It is my view that, amongst the economically developed nations, the indigenous businesses of Britain have been some of the slowest to learn and to adapt, and particularly to invest for the longer term. In the post-war years, Britain's available capital seems to have been applied, not by industrialists, disproportionately to the development of other nations. This contrasts with Japan, Germany and France. Industry is not accountable for all of its problems. We might now be beginning to catch up, but we started late in the race and one of the costs is that we have lost some of the ownership.

In all countries, managers, over the decades, have operated in the context of what might be described as a 'learned response';[2] actions and attitudes are strongly influenced by historical conventions that one generation passes on to the next. It seems to me that the process of people management in Britain today is, to too great an extent, still a reflection of the learned responses originating as far back even as the industrial revolution. Managers, shareholders and unions all subconsciously play the game, continue to feed off each other and replicate the divide. What foreign investors do in their own countries is also conditioned by their own national learning processes and gives them different outcomes to those seen in Britain. It is, however, significant that, in Britain, it is the foreign investors seeking new ways and making investments for the long term that have been brave enough to allow our conventions to be challenged and change to be heralded. Perhaps they did not believe that they were themselves introducing a change in the established order of our nation. They were merely focusing on their own needs. Nevertheless, they have demonstrated through the success of their strategies that a new order of things can be adopted in Britain. It is now for British industry in the wider sense to unlearn their instilled responses and have the faith to truly move towards a new order and maybe start again, if necessary, from a 'blank sheet of paper'. We should seek, in co-operation with our workforces, ways of working that relegate the 'them and us' mentality to the 'them' being the competition and the 'us' being all of the employees in the enterprise at every level.

Towards an integrated organisation

The qualities sought by me in the people to be employed at all levels, are remarkably similar. Clearly, expertise is required, but at Toshiba factories, whether considering top management or basic shop-floor appointments, there has been an endeavour to seek unconventional and psychometrically difficult-to-measure qualities such as enthusiasm, idealism, commitment and attention to detail. To these I must add flexibility and openness of mind, to cope with the continuous need to adapt to changing circumstances in response to customer demands, new technology and the generally turbulent times.

During the early part of my career in personnel management, it was demarcation disputes – quarrels between different union factions in the same enterprise – that featured significantly in the industrial scene. Whilst it was the unions that attracted the public attention, during the same period and in subsequent decades it has been the demarcations between functions of management that have been equally or maybe more damaging . . . the 'them and us' issue again! The segmentation of functions by profession has its hazards. In Japan, because of the wider career development systems and group-focused practices, such demarcations at management or indeed at any other level are virtually non-existent.

Peter Drucker has told of a different kind of demarcation story: about surgery, which into the 17th century was performed not by physicians but by barbers. The physicians, observing a literal interpretation of their oath not to inflict bodily harm, were too 'ethical' to cut. Operations were therefore presided over by the doctor, sitting somewhat remote from the action, who told the barber what to do, sometimes in Latin, which the barber did not understand. It was the barber's fault if the patient died and the doctor's achievement if he survived. For me, the parallel that can be drawn between the physician and the so-called personnel practitioner on the one hand and the barber and line management on the other is an alarming illustration of the state of play that has undoubtedly prevailed in some organisations and led to functional separation. It may have even led to the ostracism or elimination of the personnel function. If so, justly.

The case for Personnel

Under current economic pressures, some organisations have been reconsidering whether they need personnel departments. I'm not, in theory, against this. Excellence in any function of management can be found outside the traditional areas of guardianship of those functions. What I would take issue with, however, is the notion that organisations can afford to dispense with personnel professionals . . . in much the same way as I would challenge dispensing with accounting, legal or any other professional service. Each has its contribution to make. So what contribution can personnel professionals make?

Last year, I conducted a small experiment with a group of post-graduate students. I gave them the most comprehensive list that I could put together from the most eminent sources listing all possible internal and external impacts upon an organisation and I invited them to add to that list. I then challenged them to find *one* impact for which there was *not* a human resource related impact. They failed! A simple illustration of the inseparability of the people aspect in all management issues. The process is extremely easy and can be used as a tool to assist in the clarification of roles and contributions.

If, for whatever reason, the personnel department is eliminated as such, this presupposes either a general broadening of competencies and responsibilities, or the integration of those undertaking specialist responsibilities into multi-functional teams, or a combination of both; the scenarios are not mutually exclusive. The extent to which the different roles will be adopted will depend, amongst other things, upon the size of the organisation, the nature of the team and the number of people managed. The larger each is, the more difficult it will be to adopt an all-singing-all-dancing generalist structure. The danger in devolvement is that the quality of management may sink to that learned from booklets purchased at railway, motorway or airline bookstalls. If devolvement is to take place as part of a properly thought-through policy, then it will require professionals to facilitate the process.

Experience tells me that, at the sharp end of organisations, people in the enterprise still need at least administrative support. Of the roles that line managers are happy for someone else to do, basic administration is possibly the most notable! Yet if people management is considered to be important, the following, amongst others need servicing: recruitment and selection; manpower and organisational planning; career and management development; compensation and benefit planning/co-ordination; contractual/statutory terms and procedures; health and safety; collective communication; consultation and negotiation . . . and every area on which the force of employment law has an impact. Who will do these? A committee? Shared around the team? From outside? Devolvement has its challenges. The solutions are for each organisation to find. The personnel function might find ways to make it easier for line management to have their fingers more directly on the pulse – development of better and more readily accessed information systems, for one.

The role of Personnel

Some of the toughest but most appreciative line manager 'customers' for my personnel services over the years have, at some stage in their careers, been personnel specialists themselves. And in this, there is perhaps a maxim for professionals: that in order to increase one's professional influence and standing (one definition of power) it is first necessary to give it away. This is ideally a two-way process. The 'physician' must accept more accountability – opening up his books, knowledge and skills. The 'surgeon-barber' must encourage the doctor to get closer to the action. Their contributions will then be greater than the sum of their parts . . . to the benefit of the patient! If some of what takes place is delegation, that does not mean abrogation. Learn to trust, but *also to verify*! This is back to the control issue again. Personnel people who appear to be hanging on to vestiges of power, especially when hiding behind personnel-speak and other displays of mystique should, I suggest, be subjects for a review of their contributions.

Although this piece is about people management in the early 1990s, there is nothing new about the concept of line management accountability for personnel management. Sir Pat Lowrie, during the early 1980s, when Director of Industrial Relations for British Leyland and before he became President of the Institute of Personnel Management some years later, was quoted as saying: 'Over the last 10 or 20 years, line management has opted out of the personnel function. The attitude has been that we employ personnel managers. They should get on with it. In fact, personnel work is far too important to be left to personnel people.'

This leads me to consider what, indeed, is the role of personnel in meeting today's key business challenges? If personnel professionals surrender their wider roles and limit themselves to passively absorbing from line management those activities concerned with the nuts and bolts control, co-ordination and administration of human resources, they might feel important and needed but they will probably be so busy that they will not have much time for planning, strategic analysis, and more creative brain storming and thinking. Therefore, when such activities do take place, those individuals will not be in any position to contribute in an effective way. They might not even be involved and, if they are, they will probably not be listened to.

The prospects for the role of Personnel can be identified and more widely accepted through an analysis of the HR impact of internal and external organisational pressures, along the lines of the task given to the post-graduate students mentioned earlier (this time, however, in a more constructive way), carried out *jointly* within the extended team. The analysis needs to follow through to acceptance of the areas of human resource effectiveness and who is accountable for what. It needs to focus on specific unambiguous criteria for measuring each of the outputs. If post-graduate students, many with little industrial experience, can identify the human resource implications for any given business occurrence, then it is surely not beyond the ability of those with considerable experience and training to focus on the important points and the outputs required.

The strategic approach

It is probably not surprising that my view is that personnel should be pre-eminently concerned with creating the internal climate necessary for the organisation to meet today's key business challenges and, in particular, the climate which enables the organisation to attract, train and motivate the people that they need now and in the future. Personnel specialists will, as reviewed above, enhance both their own credibility and the organisation's performance if they concentrate more on facilitating management-in-general's capacity to implement human resource related action. Businesses, government departments and other organisations are becoming more customer focused than ever they have been in Britain. Companies aim to match their products and services to what their customers want and need. Why should not the personnel function apply this principle internally? Every department and function has internal customers! Of course, the 'proof of the pudding' is not in the making but in the eating . . . as well as, perhaps, in the digesting! Good intentions and even good practices are not ends in themselves. Good results are the evidence required, and it is for each organisation to judge what its needs are. However, if the nature of the contributions is not fully understood, the people making them will inevitably be under-recognised. If the individuals and the function are not recognised, it is difficult for them to be valued. The initiatives for recognition rest with the professionals.

Earlier, I made a reference to a strategic role. Does the personnel professional have a role, or does the premise that strategic human resource management is too important to be left to him or her hold water? This is not an either/or question: the answer to both points is '**Yes**'. If a so-called professional tries to hang on to everything, in my view this emphasises their unprofessionalism. If the processes outlined above for identifying operational and job outputs is applied at a high enough level and as part of a corporate strategic review of the business, it seems inevitable that a strategic need for a personnel professional to contribute at the highest level will emerge. Even in apparently simpler and smaller structures, the need for someone, not necessarily on a full-time basis, will become clear.

If there are already specialists in the business, it is quite appropriate for the top personnel professional to be prompting a review of the organisation and particularly the personnel function. Since every impact upon the organisation has some human resource related implication, it seems inconceivable that an organisation should not have these issues brought into focus at board level within a specialist personnel (or perhaps wider) portfolio. If, on top of responsibility for cultural and other organisational process strategies, the personnel specialist is also accountable for the standards of human resource management practised by line managers, that will be quite fitting. But to justify that role at all levels of the organisation, it is necessary to examine whether or not those undertaking the roles are indeed the 'professionals' that they may profess themselves to be. The individual, not the role, should be questioned. The valued performer will be quite apparent.

The right people for the right job

We need also to consider what breadth and depth of personal education and development will enable an individual to be best placed to respond to the kind of challenges that may be thrown up in these discontinuous and turbulent times. Dr Jonathan Miller, who originally trained as a medical practitioner, was not to my knowledge formally trained as a theatrical director, and John Elliott-Gardiner, eminent as a conductor of choral works, started in quite a different field. Patrick Moore, as an amateur, gained international eminence as an astronomer before developing further as a television personality. All are people who have reached the top in their professions. It is, with some limitations, possible to reach professional pinnacles by non-standard means. The personnel profession is no exception. However, as an aside, I hope that if I have to have surgery, the surgeon will have qualified other than as a musician or barber!

It is for those in each organisation to decide upon the capabilities, the education and the training they require of their personnel specialists, and also whether there is a place for standards of conduct, professional ethics, etc. It is worth taking into account individuals who:

- have, on top of a more general education, undertaken years of preparation for their roles, with independent scrutiny against published standards of ability and knowledge;
- accept that their conduct and work standards are subject to a code of professional ethics with disciplinary penalties for breach;
- in order to maintain and to upgrade their accreditation, need to demonstrate continuing professional development.

Individuals who have followed such a path will indicate something to me about their approach and their attitudes. I will also be able to rely upon at least their fundamental

capability. The rest will be up to them to satisfy my requirements for other and wider qualities, mentioned earlier. They
will of course be in competition with others . . . there are no
guaranteed tickets, for people or for businesses!

Capability management

In considering the subject of people management today, it
would have been tempting to go to the heart of today's more
topical issues. I have addressed flexibility and I would reiterate
the need to use our current advantages responsibly and in ways
that will enhance our enterprises and industry in the longer
term. It is no use having the cheapest and most flexible
workforce in Europe if that workforce doesn't have the
capability and motivation to work together effectively. Furthermore, with outsourcing and other such flexible practices of
working, teams may now include people not directly employed
by the organisation. They must be enjoined to the organisational
objectives as much as the 'insiders'.

Capability management is what personnel professionals
need to be about; to help create organisations that are
designed to respond smoothly to discontinuous economic and
political events. Linear planning which simply extrapolates
historical results, is no longer suitable. In considering our
capabilities for now and for the future we must openly and
honestly acknowledge the blockages to success that have
marred our performance in the past and find new ways to avoid
not only repeating the difficulties of the past but also the new
and as yet unidentified difficulties of the future. This will
certainly not be achieved by adopting the latest flavour of
instant fix, but rather by surveying our foundations and
appropriately propping them up or renewing them, and by
structuring and 'conditioning' organisations to have the capability to cope with that yet to unfold. People-led organisational
transformations that both acknowledge and value the indi-

vidual and the collective contributions of all of the employees at every level, will help build the necessary bridges.

It is open to personnel professionals to take a lead in this. If we don't, we will deserve to lose the credibility we claim in matters of people management. I have indicated that creation of the responsive 'climate', for me, comes ahead of organisational objectives. Yet the two are inextricably linked and the process can, if wished, be started from the standpoint of organisational goals. One will ultimately be led back, however, to the need to focus on the basic attitudes of all the people in the organisation. So why not start there in the first place?

References

1 Michael WHITE and Malcolm TREVOR, *Under Japanese Management: the experience of British workers*. PSI/Heinemann, 1983.
2 Bryan SADLER, *Patriotism and Profit: an occidental view of Britain's inability to emulate Japan's economic performance*. Lecture for Hosei University, June 1993.

♟ Targeting for Success at Manchester Airport

Laurence Jackson

In 1993, Manchester Airport faced an unusual dilemma: consistently the fastest growing and most profitable of the major western European airports during the 1980s, it had just won the coveted 'Silver Globe' – the Travel Industry's award for the best UK airport – for the third year in succession, and once again record profits were projected.

Many businesses would undoubtedly envy this. Yet it was this very success, and the recognition of a much more challenging trading environment, that threatened the continued profitable growth of the company. Massive debt charges for the new show-piece international terminal and rail link seemed likely to overburden the profit and loss account; profit margins were being squeezed on all sides; environmental issues were becoming increasingly demanding; and the whole nature of civil aviation in Europe was changing dramatically as the single market brought about deregulation, eased frontier controls and threatened the revenues from duty-free sales.

Things could not continue as they were. There had to be changes, and changes that went to the very root of the organisation, if it was to survive and continue to act as a powerful force for the economic regeneration of the North of England.

The key was to identify the business culture that would be appropriate for success in this more turbulent environment and to define the changes in skills, attitudes and behaviour necessary to bring about this change in culture. It was also important to gain shared understandings at all levels by communicating the new values often and with conviction and to devise strategies that would achieve the required change by building

73

on the commitment, skills and loyalty of the employees, thereby retaining the critical motivational factors that ensure consistently high levels of customer satisfaction and operational integrity. In short, it was only through considered HR strategies that the company would achieve its ambitious goals.

However, for the HR function this represented a high-risk strategy. The major changes needed would be unpopular and lead to tensions and uncertainty that could unsettle the organisation. And from previous experience I knew that, in any change situation, for every champion of the new order there are at least ten others dedicated to defending the past.

Personnel: philosophy in action

I have always maintained that for any organisation its people are the key to future business success. However, although many organisations talk of employees as their 'greatest asset', in practice the values and behaviour within those organisations do not always match up to such statements. It was my task to ensure that, if the airport made such a statement, the deeds matched the words.

When the airport's top management critically reviewed the business mission and objectives in early 1991, a set of company values was defined that would inform and underpin the strategy of the business and determine the behaviours and culture that distinguished the company from its competitors. These represented enduring value statements in relation to our *customers* ('our most important job is to serve our customers'), *excellence* ('our standard of quality; nothing less will do'), *environment* ('remaining environmentally responsible in all that we do'), *safety* ('must never be compromised') and *profitability* ('to ensure the business thrives and grows').

Paramount amongst these was the *people* value. This factor would be the ultimate differentiator between the long-term success or failure of the business, and the company's mission statement endorsed this:

> Our future success depends upon the teamwork, skill and dedication of our people. We recognise the importance of each individual's contribution and are committed to fairness and continuous personal development.

Such a policy meant a considered investment in our people to ensure that this potential was unlocked. It was vital that a strategy and action plan should be devised that would integrate with the other key strategic programmes.

The crucial consideration was that this should not represent an afterthought, reacting to financial models, business development plans and capital programmes, but that the strategic development of the business would be achieved through the conscious involvement and planning of human resources. The people value had to be visibly embodied in both the company's long-range planning and its day-to-day activities, and the HR strategy was devised in such a way that it:

- integrated with overall business strategy;
- facilitated the achievement of business objectives;
- empowered managers and enthused the workforce.

An audit of current HR initiatives indicated that programmes were already underway to address the new challenges facing the business. The performance management process was being thoroughly overhauled in line with new structures and values; individual and team skills were being developed in formal training programmes; a range of measures had been introduced to create a more participative and involved workforce; industrial relations procedures and structures were in the process of dramatic transformation; and longer-term strategies were under consideration for succession planning, pay and benefits and internal communications.

However a more profound and fundamental theme was

emerging from the communication and consideration of the 'people value'. In short, there developed a vision of the future airport workforce that envisaged all employees in one team. This was characterised by:

- a single-status agreement, with core terms and conditions harmonised;
- incentives to achieve excellence in customer service;
- low unit costs and high productivity;
- fair and consistent treatment for all;
- excellent internal communications;
- participation by all employees in decisions affecting their future.

The looming problems

Emerging from a period of record growth and enviable profitability, the company was aware that a number of factors were going to present major obstacles in the short- and medium-term future. In essence, the company had to become more **customer-centred**, consciously work to change the existing **internal culture**, and **restructure** the business to reduce base costs and to reflect its new orientation and values. It needed to adopt a more sensitive **business strategy** in response to more turbulent markets, seek to work with the key players in its external **environment** and create a framework for sustainable and **profitable growth** under a harsher funding and economic regulation regime.

In HR terms, the challenge was to ensure that the organisation adapted to a new culture and structure in a planned way. The very real dangers in this were either a rejection of new systems and approaches or an over-enthusiastic attempt to move too quickly – with the concomitant danger of cynicism, confusion and opportunism by the trade unions. In the event, this proved to be a very real concern.

Customers

The most significant change in business thinking was the new importance attached to customers. As an organisation that had demonstrated technical excellence and generated profits through shrewd and aggressive marketing based on a favourable geographical catchment area, the airport had served its prime customers (the airlines, travel trade and cargo operators) without ever fully embracing the concept of a genuine partnership. The realisation dawned, however, that a sense of partnership was imperative if we were to deliver a top-quality service to all airport users.

Equally, the vital 'internal service chain' had not been universally appreciated, with many managers of support services not being clearly aware of who their customers were, and what criteria should be used to assess their contribution to overall business success.

Internal culture

The business had grown dramatically during the previous decade. However, it was recognised that the behaviour and attitudes that had served to fuel that success were not an appropriate blueprint for the more challenging and competitive times that lay ahead. Indeed, some aspects of the internal culture were acknowledged as counter-productive to the company's stated mission and objectives.

In order to assess the nature of the shift required, a review was undertaken amongst senior management. This revealed that the company needed to convert:

- a *business orientation* that was often internally focused to one that was more customer driven;
- a *workforce* that was not always receptive to change to one that was committed and empowered to embrace new ideas;
- a *management approach* that tended to rely on dealing

(very effectively) with unexpected events and problems to a more anticipatory and strategic style;

- *standards* of service delivery that were not always quantified and monitored to ones that would ensure a competitive edge in all areas of activity;
- an *internal climate* that was highly competitive and bordered on the divisive to one that was more collaborative and involving;
- a *business culture* that was dynamic and fast moving to a more strategically driven style of organisation.

Structure

Although the current functional structure had served the company well in the five years since the company was set up, it had a number of serious shortcomings which were increasingly affecting the airport company's ability to respond quickly and effectively to problems and opportunities. These included trends towards:

- each Directorate becoming a 'power block' to be defended at all costs, thus entailing the involvement of virtually every Directorate at every stage of even the simplest of projects;
- duplications of functions: this was costly and slowed up decision-making; it also meant that there was no single point of contact for our customers;
- a widely accepted recognition that there could at times be an over-emphasis on competitiveness between the six functional Directorates;
- blurring of accountability and an unsatisfactory interface between policy/strategy formulation on the one hand and implementation/service delivery on the other.

Business strategy

To support the new approach, the company had to embrace a more strategic approach to forecasting and planning its business. Historically, the airport had projected its business plans and infrastructure development programmes on the basis of past performance and predicted industry trends. However, in the early 1990s, we began to realise that, however skilled our forecasters were, the markets were becoming more complex. Pure passenger numbers (for example) were not sufficient for planning purposes: we had to know the proportion of business and leisure travellers; which were travelling 'point-to-point' and which were transferring en route to other destinations; which were UK, which intra EC and which outside the EC; whether aircraft would become larger or smaller, etc.

Even if market segmentation analysis gave us a clearer view of this, events did not seem to conform to predictions. The increase in competition as a result of the completion of the EC internal market on 1 January 1993, changes in the industry generally, and the impact of the general economic recession – all meant that the business had to be developed in a less prescriptive way. A further burden was the imposition of a tight economic regulation regime by the Civil Aviation Authority following an investigation by the Monopolies and Mergers Commission. This meant, in effect, that our prime source of revenue (aviation charges) would show little or no increase until at least the end of the century. As a result, it was essential to develop additional commercial sources of income to supplement the core business revenues.

Environment

The company's ambitious future development plans represented both a boost to the regional economy and a potential threat to its environmental harmony and eco-systems. The problems of noise, airborne pollution and physical expansion were becoming increasingly prominent when seeking approval for capital infrastructure projects. There is no doubt that the Second Runway proposals, already the source of significant concern on the part of local action groups, will be the subject of a public enquiry. In addition, new EC legislation requires stringent environmental impact assessments to be carried out on all projects. Therefore, the only way for the business to develop was in harmony with the surrounding community, rather than in spite of it.

Framework for future growth

The company's ability to generate the revenues necessary for future investment was by no means certain. Financial projections to the year 2005 highlighted potential problems with cash flow, gearing and sources of funding. Until the new terminal and rail link began to generate a healthy return on the £250m-plus investment, there would be a crucial need to improve internal cost-effectiveness and to plan prudently for long-term success.

Coping strategies

Faced with such challenges, the board decided to adopt an integrated approach, which would ultimately transform the whole business culture. This comprised:

- a **service quality** delivery programme – 'Building the Best';
- changes to **structures, systems and learning programmes**;
- initiatives which would transform **working practices and productivity**;
- a new focus for **business strategy** that would integrate key areas of activity towards long-term company goals.

Building the best

We recognised that, in an industry like ours, service quality is probably the only sustainable source of competitive advantage.

Research showed that to satisfy our customers we had to create partnerships both internally (between our employees at all levels and in all sections) and externally (with our trading partners and suppliers). In short, we needed to continually reduce our operating costs, while at the same time raising our efficiency and the quality of service.

I knew that this was not something that we would achieve by sending round encouraging leaflets to employees, nor even by a conventional 'training event'. It was a fundamental message that we had to get across to all employees so that they understood, believed, and became enthusiastic about the process. In addition to raising understanding of our customers' needs and service standards, we knew that we had to begin to break down a fairly hostile internal climate by making every employee feel valued and involved in the exercise.

Our solution was to set up a series of one-day events, which involved 1,460 employees attending in mixed groups (50 per event) over a continuous period from 26 January to 21 February, including weekends and four night shifts. We trained two teams of presenters, involving over 50 employees in the design and delivery of the programme. Once *every* employee had taken part, we then ran a series of similar days for our customers. Above all, as we went through, we *listened* to what people said, and we have now begun to act on the outcomes.

The major benefits perceived by most participants were the opportunity to meet with a cross-section of employees who would not normally come together in the course of work, and to be able to discuss with management issues of company policy, areas of concern and customer perceptions and needs. On analysing the feedback, many similarities came out between employee and customer views. Both groups, for example, felt that communications between the company and themselves were at times poor and that they were not consulted early enough about decisions that directly affected them. There were also concerns about the visibility of management, barriers that existed between and within departments, and special problems encountered by shift and night workers. Both groups felt uncertain about service standards, and there were criticisms of the cost-reduction programmes, which were considered to have been insensitively handled. There was also a considerable degree of scepticism that the whole exercise was yet another example of 'window dressing', and that no follow up action would be taken.

As a result of the exercise, a number of measures have been taken to address these areas of concern, most notably the prominence now given in the Business Plan to developing a service quality strategy in partnership with other organisations at the airport. There have also been improvements to the team briefing and internal communications processes, the setting-up of a monthly 'Directors Question Time', improvements to facilities and amenities, and a whole series of seminars, secondments and visits designed to improve understanding and awareness throughout the business. However, it is clear that the momentum gained as a result of this has to be carefully maintained if the cynics are not to be proved correct.

Changes to structures, systems and learning programmes

Our approach to service quality had recognised the dramatic growth that the airport had experienced over the last decade and the need to take stock of our customers' expectations. Similarly, the internal structures and processes of the company had to be re-examined. We knew that a quality culture would only flourish if we had the right ingredients in both our management approach and supporting systems.

We had defined a challenging new mission 'to be the best world airport', and itemised the values that would ensure that this could be achieved. We now had to ensure that the structure of the business would make it easy to deliver quality, that supporting processes were in place to guarantee excellence in service, and that we could develop the competence of each individual to fulfil his or her role fully effectively. Above all, and more subtly than these technical and programme changes, we needed to adopt a conscious leadership style that would empower all employees to give of their best.

We had already embarked on a major restructuring of the business. The whole focus of the business was shifted towards customer service and delivery by establishing three major self-standing businesses to which other departments provided services. Innovative thinking was to be encouraged, and a framework for long-term growth and succession established.

To support this, business centre accounting was introduced, and management information became a priority for the improvement of existing monitoring and reporting systems. The benefits of this showed through in terms of improved customer satisfaction and increased internal efficiency. There was a dramatic and permanent reduction of over £1m per annum in base costs through the elimination of duplication and the rationalisation of processes, and the old unhelpful barriers that had grown up under the former structure began to be broken down.

We now recognised the need to provide support and development opportunities for managers in new and (in many cases) bigger jobs. The highly effective competency-based management development programme, introduced in 1988, had established a shared common framework within the company. This enabled performance to be reviewed and expectations to be communicated to jobholders in a language that everyone understood. Originally designed as a process for identifying development needs and to encourage and facilitate personal learning, it was now used as a basis for analysing and evaluating jobs, conducting more effective appraisals, setting performance standards, giving constructive feedback, and predicting who had the capacity for bigger jobs.

As people were appointed to new jobs, priority was given to defining the immediate and medium-term expectations within the job. Personal Learning Plans were then agreed that would enable each employee to develop skills and know-how in the

specific competences that were most critical to their performance in the new job. This has proved to be not only an
extremely effective learning process, but also very valuable for
analysing job requirements and discussing performance expectations in an open and supportive way.

Working practices and productivity

In the major areas of service delivery, extensive reviews of
working practices and resource allocation were undertaken
with the aim of improving productivity and cost-effectiveness.
The new international terminal, opened in March 1993,
provided the opportunity to review resourcing arrangements in
all sections, and significant savings were achieved through
collaborative exercises in engineering, security and car parks.
Multi-skilling and the introduction of annual hours enabled
both terminals to be maintained and serviced with virtually the
same engineering staff numbers as for one; and the new
agreements in security and car parks ensured that, despite the
significant increase in services provided and areas covered, the
base budget for employee costs in 1993/94 was actually less
than the out-turn employee costs for the previous year.

Business strategy

A top management workshop analysed the issues facing the
business and the strategies needed to secure competitive
advantage and the achievement of the business mission and
objectives. This resulted in a refocusing of the company's core
business strategy, both in aviation and in the increasingly
important commercial revenues, a major new environmental
strategy, and a serious reconsideration of the funding necessary
to finance the anticipated capital programmes, including the
second runway project needed by 1997.

The common theme emerging from all of these exercises was
the critical role of our workforce in addressing the challenges

ahead. The 'Building the Best' workshops had created the platform – raising awareness and putting customers in the spotlight. We knew that our employees were prepared to 'go the extra mile', but that we had to involve them more in decisions affecting their future, communicate with them more frequently and purposefully, and take action to redress concerns and shortcomings.

This demanded from top management a type of leadership that would inspire and enthuse, rather than simply enforce and monitor. We knew that the traditional 'command and control' leadership style, one that had proved effective in the past, was no longer compatible with the concept of freeing up individuals to strive for continuous improvements in service. The emphasis was now to be on encouraging and supporting, illustrating the way, and coaching rather than telling.

Bridging the communication gap

Perhaps the greatest difficulty we faced was communicating the seriousness of the issues facing the business, although this was vital to establishing the rationale for an organisational restructuring and action plan that would affect every employee. With business throughput continuing to defy trends in the economy generally, record profits projected, and confirmation from our customers that we were perceived as the top UK airport, it was genuinely difficult to persuade even senior managers that changes were necessary. Indeed, for many who had been successful under the existing regime, such changes represented not just a disruption, but a positive threat to future career progression. In addition, there was initial scepticism and resistance from some of the recognised trade unions, who quite naturally sought to protect the interests of employees who might be adversely affected by any changes in structure, and who wished to make attendance at the service quality seminars voluntary.

In the circumstances, it would have been easier for management to allow exceptions, provided that the majority of the workforce co-operated. However we recognised the danger of an 'opt out' clause, since it would in effect confirm the old values and negate any concerted effort to introduce the attitudes, behaviours and approaches which the new culture required.

As a result, it had to be established from the outset that every employee would participate in the process – not under compulsion, but because it was a reasonable requirement of their employment. If they were to believe this, then the message had to come from their own manager or supervisor – some of whom felt equally anxious and apprehensive about the whole process. This demanded a thorough and systematic communications exercise to explain why the business would not prosper without such changes. It was also necessary to reassure everyone that management would genuinely listen to employees and act on any issues of concern that emerged, and that arrangements were in place to deal sensitively and fairly with any employees disadvantaged as a result of the restructuring.

In the event, there was a largely positive response to the 'Building the Best' seminar, although there were instances where employees attended without really participating and some feelings still remain that real issues were not properly addressed.

Effective decision-making

The organisation had always had to respond rapidly and effectively to unexpected events, quite often at night or weekends. Airport management had developed a capacity to take appropriate decisions on a whole range of operational and tactical issues, at times involving major sums of money. After all, a 15-minute delay in loading bags onto an aircraft could result in that aircraft missing its 'slot time' for departure, and hence potentially incurring massive additional costs and problems. The cost of indecision to our customers could be great. Therefore, there had to be a delegation of authority to supervisors and managers to enable continuity of service to be maintained. However, as the airport grew, it became increasingly difficult to co-ordinate such actions from the centre. It was evident that there was a need for a more systematic approach to decision-making, and a better framework within which authority could be delegated.

The formal authorisation process ('Scheme for delegation of authority') was reviewed, and the limits and approvals necessary critically reconsidered in the light of the new structure. Interestingly, it emerged that management already had adequate powers to commit expenditure and take decisions. What they lacked was the confidence that they were acting in accordance with company regulations, and the certainty that their decisions would always be supported. In order to give our employees this confidence, we had first of all to establish clarity of purpose and direction, and then to communicate this widely so as to achieve a shared understanding amongst all the workforce. In order to empower our employees to deliver high quality we needed to delegate responsibility, and the whole had to be reinforced by a new style of leadership from top management. These then became the 'keys' to effective decision-making.

Clarity of purpose and direction

In redefining its mission and values, the company had made very positive statements about what we stand for, what we are setting out to achieve, and how are we going to get there. These straightforward but powerful statements became the priorities that determine actions at the key point of achievement, and had to be robust enough to survive over time.

Communicating and reinforcing

In order to ensure that the new approach was fully understood and widely shared, an extensive programme of internal communications was undertaken. The core of this was a series of 'cascade' briefings whereby managers took their subordinates through the ideas and allowed time for debate, challenge and reflection. This was reinforced by articles in the employee newspaper, personal letters to all employees and special events.

Delegating responsibility

Much has been written about 'empowerment' – and it is rightly perceived as a very effective process for ensuring high-quality service delivery. It was our view that this should extend not just to improved communication and consultation, and increases in authority to spend; we believe strongly that those whose job it is to deliver and improve the service to our customers must not only have the skills, but also the freedom and confidence to do so. Jobs were redesigned on this principle, layers streamlined, and employees were encouraged to participate in decisions about their unit's performance and the thinking about the future.

It was without doubt right to embark on this process; and there were examples of employees who eagerly grasped the opportunity to take decisions which improved customer service and generated compliments where previously we had been accustomed to complaints. In one instance, a passenger whose problem was resolved by the prompt actions of a supervisor turned out to be a top manager from a major customer, who was very favourably impressed.

But we also came to realise very quickly that a superficial understanding of empowerment could actually be counter-productive. On learning of their new-found freedoms, managers were tempted to rush off and order new equipment, make special awards to their staff or give authorisations outside the company's agreed terms. We had to move quickly to clarify this before anarchy broke out.

More significantly, in HR terms, a new tension arose between 'the centre', where group policy was determined, and the newly established HR functions in the businesses. The role of a central HR presence was questioned as local deals were struck and new approaches evolved. Whilst this undoubtedly benefited the individual businesses there was a danger of inconsistency of approach, leading to concerns about fairness, and the very real risk of being exploited by shrewd shop stewards who sought to capitalise on the 'highest common denominator' in comparability claims.

The organisation is coming to terms with this through regular liaison between all the HR sections, thereby evolving a new *modus operandi* to ensure that the new businesses do benefit from more autonomy without compromising corporate standards or the overall effectiveness of policy implementation.

Leadership style

In order to bring about a quality culture, we needed to develop leaders. It was therefore fundamental that we examined and challenged the current style of leadership within the organisation. There were elements of organisational style which we knew were not conducive to developing the new culture. We diagnosed, for example, defensive behaviours, a refusal to admit to mistakes for fear of retribution, an insistence on 'one right way to do things' (usually the leader's own), the development of 'empires', frequent conflict between sections and departments, and people rarely being congratulated or praised for their achievements. This climate led to enormous frustration and waste, and tended to disempower both the leader and his or her team. What we needed to cultivate now was a style which:

- *challenged the process* – searching for opportunities, experimenting and being prepared to take risks;
- *inspired a shared vision* – picturing the future and enlisting others;
- *enabled others to act* – fostering collaboration and strengthening others;
- *modelled the way* – setting the example and planning small successes;
- *won hearts and minds* – recognising individual contributions and celebrating accomplishments.

Of course it is simplistic to assume that long-ingrained habits will change overnight. Indeed, it is extremely difficult to adopt a new style, especially when the previous approach has appeared to be effective and endorsed by the company's formal and informal reward system.

When we considered this with our senior managers, we found that their greatest concern was that there was never going to be enough time to meet all the demands of their job, let alone become more strategic. There was clear evidence that several of them were overworking to the point of self-sacrifice, where they were becoming unfit and incapable of leading. In order to make time for themselves they needed to delegate. However this required them to have confidence in their subordinates. To gain this confidence they had to devote time to the development of skills and competencies in their teams. This involved a coaching and mentoring approach which has proved extremely helpful in ensuring that the capacity of employees is both recognised and developed.

Rethinking the organisational style

The competency-based management development programme has had a dramatic impact on the management style and culture of the organisation.

The characteristics which had brought success in the 1980s were no longer appropriate for the more turbulent and competitive environment within which the business now operates. We have successfully converted technical experts into skilled business managers and developed the strategic thinking capacity of those whose response was always reactive and often punitive. Managers who were skilled in exploiting the bureaucratic systems of a heavily local-government orientated organisation have learned to become accountable decision-makers; and we have reinforced and encouraged collaborative activity and participation rather than the divisive behaviours which tended to be prevalent previously.

As we have reviewed the competency profile most likely to be indicative of success in the current climate, the importance of 'customer orientation' has been dramatically enhanced; all employees must be sensitive to customer needs and responsive in meeting them. A sound understanding of modern business practices has also emerged as a more significant requirement for our management. But above all, we need all our employees to recognise the importance of personal learning as the key to personal effectiveness and future development. Managers must set the example – encouraging, supporting and taking a genuine interest in the improvement in skills and competencies of all of their teams.

Personnel: a role in the boardroom?

The question of personnel representatives at board level has exercised many people within and outside the profession. Whilst 'a seat on the board' may not be the norm for Personnel in most organisations, it remains evident that the human resource strategy is an intrinsic element of any organisation's thinking at the highest level. Indeed, at the airport, although the Personnel Director has never been a board member in the sense of having voting rights, there has consistently been a requirement for him to attend board meetings because of the significance of personnel considerations to the items on the agenda.

As in most organisations, the major expense is employee costs. Therefore the effective strategic management of these resources is vital to achieving the company's objective. The key contributions of Personnel at board level are to help develop the company's capacity to think and operate strategically, to identify the composition and nature of the workforce required five and ten years ahead and devise appropriate resourcing programmes, and to advise on the important legal or other considerations in relation to planned business developments.

In the past where such matters have only been considered after major policy decisions have been taken, the outcome has tended to be more problematical, and in many cases more expensive. However, it is also clear that under a regime where more authority is delegated to front-line businesses, HR has a more difficult task in influencing line managers to take a strategic line in their decision-making processes.

Personnel: meeting today's business challenges

The business plan prepared for the trading year commencing 1st April 1993 exemplifies the very real contribution which personnel makes.

The Chief Executive's introduction states Manchester Airport's firm resolve to become a world leader in service quality. He continues that 'service quality can *only* be delivered by a continued commitment to developing our people'. This theme is continued in the body of the plan, in which one of the major business priorities for 1993/94 is an integrated programme to 'make new teams more effective'. This involves a whole range of measures designed to develop key business competencies, introduce a new performance management system, harmonise terms and conditions of employment, rationalise recognition and collective bargaining arrangements, implement team building programmes, improve internal communications and develop the new organisation.

All of these have to be addressed if the progress made over the last eighteen months is to be maintained. Indeed, under the other four business priorities (which have either a technical or a financial bias), there are frequent references to employee considerations 'improving communications', 'establishing service quality partnerships', 'set-up service improvement teams, 'joint training ventures', 'improve productivity' etc.). Quite clearly, it is not just ensuring the appropriate resourcing that is important but improving skills at all levels, creating the right climate and enthusing employees to deliver high-quality service on a cost-effective basis.

The years ahead

As the business contemplates further major infrastructure development to position the airport as a world operator, the strategic issues begin to be defined: an increasing focus on the environment and community; closer alliance in socio-economic and cultural terms within the European Community; and an ever tougher trading environment.

In Personnel terms, the challenges will be to retain Manchester's competitive edge in its chosen markets through developing genuine internal and external partnerships. It will also be important to ensure that the appropriate skills are available within the workforce in order to keep ahead of changes in the external environment, and to create and sustain an internal climate whereby all employees identify strongly with the organisation, are proud of their job, and are determined to give of their best to provide an excellent service.

Conclusion

The past twelve months have seen massive changes affecting everyone who works for the airport company. Change is not always welcome, and for many it has been a period of uncertainty and anxiety that they would not wish to re-live. However, the signs are positive: the organisation is sharper, more focused on customers and productivity is dramatically improved. Customers have expressed their satisfaction with the new order, and business throughput continues to show very healthy trends, with the new international terminal and rail link attracting accolades from all quarters.

A rigorous analysis of the company's position and its prospects has underlined the fact that, although massive technical, environmental and financial challenges face the business, its people will continue to play an absolutely crucial role in developing the business to meet customers' expectations. This has reinforced the message that the airport must continue to devise strategies to involve employees at all levels in operations, business strategy and planning, so as to ensure that it can attract, retain, motivate and develop the high performers in all functions, and so ensure the continued growth and success of the business.

Don't Forget the Engine Room

Janet Rubin

Two interpretations of the title of this book occur to me – both pertinent to the personnel function. A 'view from the bridge' could refer to a crossing over a river, say, or the command position on a ship. However, if our view is from the river crossing, do we look upstream to see where we have been or do we look downstream, to the future, to where we should be going? On the other hand, a 'view from the bridge' of a ship is important for setting and monitoring the course. Naturally, Personnel has to have influence here; but the view within and from the engine room is equally important.

This latter 'view from the bridge' emphasises, for me, some of the critical issues for the personnel function, both now and for the next three to five years: the need to be forward looking, dealing with strategic issues, facilitating the process of change, but not forgetting the people who drive and support the business. This means ensuring that there is positive teamwork so that the whole is greater than the sum of the parts. Through this active 'view from the bridge', Personnel will ensure that there is no doubt about its added value.

Theory and practice

I start from the position that the people who work in an organisation still represent a huge and largely untapped resource but also constitute a major challenge. Markets and products are becoming global and subject to increasingly rapid change, and any technological advance is quickly matched. Managing people effectively, however, is a skill which is not so easily copied and is therefore, in Michael Porter's words, a source of sustainable competitive advantage.

95

My underlying personnel philosophy, therefore, is that the personnel function must contribute to business performance in ways which can be measured as well as in qualitative terms. The Personnel Lead Body statement, *A Perspective on Personnel*, contains a good definition of what all of us are trying to achieve.

> The key purpose of Personnel is to . . . enable management to enhance the individual and collective contributions of people to the short- and long-term success of the enterprise.

However, Personnel can be an uncomfortable function to be in – one in which everyone regards themselves as experts, where the boundaries are at times unclear and where one is often dealing with largely qualitative and sensitive issues. I have heard the function called 'the organisation's conscience' and I have been described by a previous managing director as the 'shop steward on the board'. At times I have been obliged to confront my colleagues with uncomfortable issues, for example:

– Are we really operating as a team?
– Is our behaviour in line with the standards and policies we have set ourselves and publicised?
– Are we really listening to our employees, even when they say things we would prefer not to hear?

In W H Smith, the Group Personnel's vision is:

> To create and maintain an environment which supports and extends group culture and leadership styles. We will achieve this through our role as change agent and by creating, providing and facilitating best demonstrated practice to optimise business performance. We will aim to be the acknowledged leader in the development of management potential and, through them, their staff. Working with businesses, the aim is to attract, train, and retain the most able staff in the industry.

One of the tasks for my department has been to take the broader corporate vision and leadership statements agreed by the board and develop from them blueprints for action which are consistent, focus on the future and mean something to our employees. These are not personnel policies. We decided that the very title 'personnel policies' sent the wrong messages; our concern is with *people*, not with policies which belong to the personnel function. To reflect this, the blueprints we have developed are called 'Management of People Statements'.

They are partly about where we want to get to and partly about how we want to get there. They also provide a benchmark for our actions. These are top-level statements. They are brief. They are intended to be easily understood and accessible. Our 'Management of People Statements' encompass, for example, management style, communications and equal opportunities. We have also produced a statement, in the context of equal opportunities, on HIV and AIDS, and are now implementing it. To help give external expression to this internal development we have supported the UK Corporate HIV and AIDS Project set up by the Terrence Higgins Trust and we are signatories of the National AIDS Trust Companies act! Charter. We see this as a matter of action reinforcing our philosophy.

Statements of intent are fine. Putting them into practice is usually much more difficult. We must encourage managers to consider 'people issues' with the same intensity as financial and customer issues. Senior personnel professionals still have their work cut out to demonstrate the direct relationship between managing people effectively and improving business performance. Yet I'm not sure that as a profession we do this with sufficient vigour.

The challenge is particularly formidable in areas such as equal opportunities, where many managers still have very strong views. Here, one way forward is to provide hard factual evidence that companies which are perceived to be equal opportunity employers are more successful in recruiting and retaining high-quality people than those which are not. However, you have also got to change hearts and minds through openly and honestly discussing attitudes and prejudices – which we all have, but need to recognise and confront.

Meeting the challenge

For the coming year, I hope that the biggest challenge will be working within an environment of faster economic growth. Business, however, is still tough. Although the underlying trend has been firmer in 1993, the pressure to control costs and improve productivity has been unrelenting. In a retail and distribution company the biggest single cost is that of employing people. A lot of effort, therefore, has had to be put in to keeping the overall pay bill under control and finding more efficient ways of doing things.

One mechanism was to delay the annual pay/salary reviews in the group's businesses by four months. In doing this, we set out to ensure that expectations were realistic and to develop an understanding that if everyone made some sacrifice on pay there should be less need to make people redundant.

In some of our markets, however, the severity of the recession has made redundancies unavoidable. It was really difficult to reduce by 20 per cent the number of people employed in the head office of a relatively young business which had never before experienced significant cuts. Although it wasn't an easy task, we tried to ensure that we carried it out in a wholly professional way – by, for example, coaching the directors on the issue, consulting on the redundancy criteria, ensuring that the redundancy payments were fair and reasonable, offering personal and job search counselling, seeking out possible job opportunities elsewhere in the group or with other employers in the locality, and generally ensuring that the logistics of the whole exercise were handled with thoroughness and care.

Reducing the cost base in other parts of the group was less

traumatic. In the retail and distribution sector, natural wastage remains high, even in a recession, so the non-replacement of leavers offered a relatively painless way forward. In other cases, branch staff agreed to take a cut in their hours of work rather than have some of their colleagues made redundant. This obviously worked wonders for team-building but still caused some pain in an industry where wages and salaries are relatively modest.

Towards the end of 1992, the Group's Management Development Centre stopped running courses for three months so that people stayed at work in the businesses during key sales periods. However, there was the secondary benefit of saving the money that would have been incurred in course overheads.

We have also looked at our structures and removed some management tiers, and at the same time given increased accountability to those remaining.

Managing the morale of our workforce was also a challenge. As a Group, we were not in a catastrophic situation and we did not want our people to feel that business was worse than it was. However, this recession has taken its toll of people in terms of work demands and stress, as the recent *Employment in Britain Survey* has shown, and the Group was no exception.

Another crucial response to the recession on the part of all our businesses has been to increase productivity. This has occurred through reducing the number of people employed and by organising work differently. Some of this has come through reorganising the way we work, throughout our companies, as a result of measuring processes and resources. We have, for example, made greater use of part-time staff, a trend which has been developing for some years as a means of improving customer service while at the same time controlling the cost base. There are real benefits for our businesses in achieving a closer match between staffing levels, working hours and trading needs.

Everyone talks of being 'leaner and fitter', and most of us have become so during the past two years, but fitter for *what*? Companies now emerging from the recession need to be clear about the direction in which they want to go and how they plan to get there.

The keys to effective decision-making

'Consistency of purpose,' says the old Chinese proverb, 'is the secret of success.' The first and most basic step is to prepare your case well. My team, for example, frequently have to develop and communicate ideas on subjects as varied as updates on European legislation, Sunday trading, budget changes (such as the tax implications of relocation), job advertising or job swops between the businesses. Our arguments need to be sound if we are to demonstrate and convince top management of the business benefits or risks.

In this area, my task is to provide ideas and challenge the team and to ensure that the proposals have strategic direction, are practical and meet the needs of our internal (and where possible, external) customers. This may require a return to the drawing board, but more usually revision and refinement.

The second step is to make sure the proposal is directly relevant to improving business performance. A good recent example of this has been the introduction of vision testing. Given the existence of an EC directive on the subject, as a good employer we decided to act sooner rather than later. However, it was also important that we involved our businesses in the process and ensured that testing was carried out in the most appropriate way for our many different locations. We had to do it, we had to ensure that it was done well, but we had to ensure that we controlled the cost at the same time.

I am learning (through honest feedback!) to keep such proposals short and to the point. Directors and senior managers are incredibly busy people with bulging in-trays and whose hearts tend to drop if they see a lengthy report! If, and I say that advisedly, a detailed report is absolutely necessary, then a management summary has to appear at the front.

In presenting the case, I will also try to give preferred options. We have a variety of businesses in our group, several different cultures and two joint ventures. What suits one of them does not necessarily suit the other, hence the need for some flexibility in achieving group objectives. However, we all need to buy into the underlying beliefs and values of the Group.

I will also try to ensure that we quantify the costs and benefits of our decisions. The costs, unfortunately, are often easier to quantify than the benefits. The costs of the tax changes on relocation introduced in the March 1993 budget, for example, are relatively easy to quantify. The benefits less so. However I find that this is often what senior managers and directors want to know and we fail to provide it at our peril!

It sometimes requires courage to say what the benefits will be. For example we are in the process of implementing a new Personnel Management Information System. We have said that we will get quantifiable benefits from it by reducing the levels of absenteeism and staff turnover in the group through having better information on which to take action. When you are spending millions of pounds you need to be able to justify it.

Another lesson I have learned over the past (sounding like a wise old owl!) is, wherever possible, to consult well in advance of making decisions. There are, of course, some issues on which you cannot consult everyone, or you would never make a decision: for example, if you have to make some people redundant or you need to give an opinion on a sensitive organisational issue which not all your colleagues know about. Nevertheless these exceptions tend to be relatively few and far between.

Consultation tends to mean that you end up with better solutions than you otherwise would have and, above all, that you get commitment to the solution. An example is our monthly meeting of personnel heads which involves the total personnel function in the Group. Major issues or proposals are tabled at these meetings so that the personnel heads can voice their opinions and convey those of their line colleagues on the boards of the businesses before final decisions are taken. People will also be fiercely resentful if a decision has been taken without their involvement on a matter in which they have an interest. It may be that consultation will not materially change the final decision, although if we really believe in 'empowerment' there must be at least a possibility that the process used will have some bearing on the eventual outcome.

Lobbying can also be an effective means of getting things done in the right way. Sometimes I think we in the personnel function imagine that all we need to do is make a good case, set out all the features and wait for everyone else to be convinced by the sheer weight and elegance of the argument. In reality, of course, other managers may not fully understand what is being advocated and will resist it. Line managers will have had a lot less time to think through the issues and may need a lot of persuading.

I have had recent experience of this on two occasions. The first was the introduction of a flexible benefits package for group senior managers, where the timescale eventually agreed had to be more gradual than the one we anticipated. Similarly, revising the Group's appraisal scheme is taking longer than we might have wished because my line colleagues have argued that there should be plenty of time for consultation.

The last comment I would make is more of a philosophical one. Personnel functions tend not to have to make too many decisions! By that I mean we spend much of our time influencing others so that the right decisions are achieved at the right time. It is particularly important, therefore, that we become more skilled in communicating with and persuading those who have to be influenced, and will take the final decisions.

Selection and development

This is a difficult topic, as our Group is in the midst of a three-year research study which will tell us with some precision what makes our managers successful. When available, this critical information will be incorporated into our recruitment and selection process. Like most other companies, our strategy is, wherever possible, to promote from within and 'grow our own', but it is important from the start to ensure we get the best person for the job.

However there are some existing criteria which are and will remain vital. The first is that managers must practice the style of leadership which the group has defined as part of its Vision Statement. This is easier said than done, especially if you have previously worked for a boss whose style was based on command and control.

To help managers adopt the new style we have introduced a number of training initiatives on subjects such as 'The Manager as Coach', 'Strategic Leadership', and 'Maximising the Sales Effectiveness of your Branch', which are all about motivating the people who work for you. We have also taken every opportunity on whatever training programme we have been running to explain the new leadership style and why it is relevant to business performance. We have further emphasised its importance in our current review of the Group's appraisal scheme by proposing the adoption of two 'behaviourial' objectives in addition to the more conventional task or training orientated performance criteria.

If our leadership style is to succeed our managers must also develop other qualities and skills. These include involving their people in decisions and enabling them to act. We have therefore introduced both team briefing and team listening sessions in some of our retail operations. We have also championed the introduction of a high-profile suggestion scheme in our larger business.

We are optimistic that this scheme will help us unlock the full potential of our people. Certainly the initial signs are good. In the first 60 days of its operation, 770 suggestions were received from an employee base of 14,955.

Our managers also need qualities such as intellectual strength, which we have identified as having a strong correlation with business success. They should have some affinity for people and be sensitive to others, yet at the same time be capable of being tough, sceptical and competitive. They need to be relatively relaxed and avoid becoming frustrated, self-sufficient and resourceful, open to experience and relatively extrovert.

Some of these qualities also apply to our non-managerial employees. We want to unlock their full capabilities, and I always find particularly frightening the research statistic that many people only use 20 per cent of their potential at work!

We are also improving our recruitment and selection techniques at shop floor/warehouse level where staff turnover costs the company millions of pounds. And we have carried out extensive research into the use of recruitment tests and questionnaires for sales assistants. We are about to launch a pilot study using a test aimed at identifying such factors as persuasiveness, confidence, alertness – the things that we believe make a good sales assistant.

If we can ensure that we recruit people who are relatively extrovert (and therefore do not hide behind the fixtures!), who don't get easily upset (by the general public or, at times, their boss) and who are happy and satisfied, we will have achieved what all retailers seek: a quality of service which is truly memorable and, therefore, a sustainable competitive advantage.

Personnel: a role in the boardroom?

Are people management issues critical at board level? Should the personnel function have an effective influence at board level? Should board members undertake people management responsibilities? Ask any self-respecting personnel professional any of these questions and the answer will be an emphatic 'Yes!' But this does not always imply a Personnel presence on the main board.

In the W H Smith Group our Group Personnel Director, Rodney Buse, does not sit on the board, which comprises four executive directors and seven non-executive directors. Instead, the Group Personnel Director reports to Sir Malcolm Field, the Group Managing Director, who represents the function at this level. This doesn't mean that there is an exclusion zone – quite the reverse, in fact, as Personnel is regularly asked to speak at the board on people issues.

Sir Simon Hornby, the Group Chairman, has recently taken clear and public positions on equal opportunities issues such as 'Opportunity 2000' and an HIV and AIDS employment policy. Knowing that there is strong people management support at the very top of the organisation is a great advantage to us in developing initiatives and making our case with our line and personnel manager customers.

Whether or not there needs to be a Personnel Director in the boardroom is therefore debatable. What matters is the value the board attaches to the contribution its people make to the business. The role of Personnel is to demonstrate the importance of people management issues.

If I had to make a forecast, I would say we will see more Personnel Directors in the boardroom. However, this will depend on whether organisations see the function as playing an integral part in the development of business strategy – which in turn hangs on the effectiveness with which personnel professionals communicate the strategic case. It will also depend on how main boards operate in future. If, in the light of the Cadbury Report, the composition of the board changes to include more non-executive directors, then we may not see more personnel Directors.

The role of personnel in meeting today's key business challenges

The role of Personnel is to help managers get the best out of their people. By this I mean ensuring they are highly committed to the organisation and have the opportunity to give of their best.

Employees will obviously be more committed if they know what is going on, know what the organisation is trying to achieve and find their work enjoyable. Furthermore, if we can unlock more of the potential within our people and ensure that they feel good about themselves, we will all achieve more. To help us in this we need to undertake both communication and attitude surveys to help us track how we are doing and what we need to focus on in order to improve.

Getting the best out of people also depends on how their work is organised. As I mentioned earlier, to be effective in our business we have to ensure we have the flexibility in staffing levels and in the hours of work to meet the longer trading hours expected by our customers and to respond to training peaks and troughs. Flexibility is, of course, a reciprocal advantage. We are, for example, aiming to be flexible in meeting the needs of (primarily) women returners by offering term-time contracts. W H Smith is also responding to the needs of its people by offering career breaks, job sharing and publicising vacancies within the group.

I am also a fan of flexible benefit packages for managers, which enables individuals to choose from a menu those benefits which most matter to them. Annual benefit statements are also useful in so far as they help people to appreciate the value of their total package. It is important that we are able to maximise the value of our employment costs by incorporating as much flexibility as possible, particularly when we cannot increase total remuneration very much, if at all.

Another priority for the personnel function is to ensure that the organisation treats people fairly. When there is a strong pressure to control costs, we look at how that can be done through reducing hours or delaying pay reviews, rather than making people redundant. We have to help achieve business objectives while demonstrating that people matter. How you treat anyone you have to make redundant gives very strong signals to those who remain in the organisation.

Personnel has to be aware of the changes which are happening in the market place and respond quickly. We must be able, for example, to anticipate and manage longer trading hours, whether they arise from changing social habits or the legislation on Sunday trading.

Personnel professionals must be agents of change. But, importantly, they must be good at both explaining the implications of change for people as well as managing change themselves.

Our job is to propose solutions to problems before the options become restricted. To that end, we have to be less reactive. We need, for example, to come up with responses to EC employment directives before implementation ceases to be a matter of choice. Personnel professionals should, therefore, act like external sensors – picking up issues when they are still some distance away, transmitting their presence to the corporate centre, while observing how competitors are responding and guiding the strategy of their own organisation.

If something has worked successfully elsewhere and seems relevant to one's own organisation why re-invent the wheel? I am reminded of Tom Peters' view that organisations generally don't spend enough time doing this external scanning. As a result, they fail either to see new competitors appearing or to diagnose changes in their marketplace. There are some major national and international names that have fallen into this trap.

The main issues for the years ahead

I would answer this question by taking a relatively short-term focus of one to three years, and here the prognosis is 'more of the same'. Trading will remain difficult and growth rates in the UK are likely to remain low with unemployment relatively high. So the main issues in these circumstances will be:

• dealing with the new UK and European employment legislation;

- continuing to increase the productivity of our people by improving the organisation and measurement of work;
- finding ways of increasing the flexibility of our workforce to meet both our needs as a business and their needs as people;
- ensuring that our customer service is better than our competitors;
- learning more about how we can release the potential within our people and putting it into practice;
- finding ways of enabling our people.

And, above all, changing our management styles, if we are to achieve all the above.

We will also continue to grapple with the challenge of how to be a low-cost operator while remaining a good employer. By good I mean offering the level of pay and benefits appropriate to a premier division employer. This is not an easy issue to resolve and can only be achieved through a combination of success in the marketplace and high levels of productivity. A lean organisation need not be a mean one.

Finally, we must continue to demonstrate that the personnel function adds value, for example:

- providing an effective internal resource, thereby avoiding the need for external consultants;
- giving practical support to line managers;
- establishing which external suppliers give the best value in search and selection, outplacement and training areas;
- facilitating skills transfer through planned career moves, management development programmes and publicising vacancies;
- involving managers in organisational effectiveness initiatives and in networking – helping them to manage change;
- continuing to tackle strategic as well as operational issues, and providing directors and line managers with 'people' solutions to business issues.

Conclusion

In conclusion I return to the nautical analogy with which I started my voyage through this chapter. As personnel professionals we are in the same boat as the other employees of our organisations; we are all part of the same crew. We can find ourselves together battling against the elements; the economic and trading oceans are not always calm. Despite all the charts and high technology navigational aids, there are occasions when it is only our training, skill, experience, judgement and teamwork that will carry us through.

Perhaps it sounds old-fashioned, but it is that combination of support and leadership that our function brings to the rest of the crew – the ability to link the requirements of the bridge with those of the engine room – that is the added value the personnel function can bring to an organisation. If the bridge doesn't talk with the engine room it doesn't know what is going on. Unlike the nautical tradition, the modern enterprise must have crew involvement rather than command and control.

When you are on the bridge, looking forward, don't forget it's the engine room that pushes the ship along!

♟ Continuity and Change in the Financial Sector

Kathryn Riley

To remain competitive, organisations need to create a culture that is client focused and client driven. The human resource (HR) function plays a pivotal role in shaping this culture, as HR mechanisms can enable the development of a responsive environment, turning the organisation outwards to create a competitive edge. The key to survival will be to develop organisational agility.

For me, this underlying personnel philosophy has not changed, irrespective of competitive pressures. The aim is to create an organisational climate that can attract, retain, motivate and develop individuals at all levels to meet the needs of the business. How we achieve this is by ensuring that core HR values are woven into business thinking and action. The essence of this can be summed up simply as maintaining the dignity and value of the individual at all times. We all know that organisations get the staff they deserve. Responsive, motivated, committed individuals are more likely to be found in organisations that are open, are supportive of their staff, encourage mutual feedback and emphasise shared values. This demands a management team which is thoughtful and sensitive to the needs of its workforce and encourages the right level of consultation and participation.

People imperatives are reflected in corporate literature, handbooks, publications, etc. However HR is the guardian of an organisation's core values and it has to challenge the organisation to maintain them. This means ensuring that the management team 'walk the talk'. An emphasis on the importance of HR issues needs to be a key element in management development training. As well as increasing line management's

110

awareness of HR issues we need to ensure that it has the necessary skills. In order to do this, HR has to be as close to the business as possible and understand those who drive it. HR can only do this if it is in partnership with line management.

Shaping the vision into reality means that HR has to be represented at main board level. HR is an integral part of the strategy and planning of business development; for example, consideration of HR issues is vital in areas such as acquisitions, divestures and internationalisation. My vision for HR has meant creating an HR platform which adds value and has an impact at the strategic level.

When I was with County NatWest, a full-service investment bank, realising this vision meant raising the profile of the HR function and achieving recognition for its pivotal role as a partner to the business divisions. The department moved from an administrative mode into one which was productive, strategic in its thinking, driven by business considerations and supportive of the plans and objectives of operating departments. The essence of our approach was the creation of a vibrant and supportive professional team. We developed our own skills base which included selling and negotiating, consultancy and team-building skills. We also developed 'Strategic Milestones'.[1] These combined a number of features: the emphasis was on output not input, it was multi-disciplinary (as the shared responsibility of the HR department as a whole), progress could be measured and results evaluated, and there was a capacity to review and update. However, the crucial element was the role of line management.

One of the key elements for the effective delivery of HR strategy is the relationship between line management and HR. Perhaps the most important result of County NatWest's Strategic Milestones exercise was to emphasise that the achievement of HR objectives was a joint task between line management and the functional specialist. The success of Strategic Milestones depended on positive support elsewhere in the organisation, and the developing of the Milestones gave

HR the opportunity to make this contingent relationship explicit.

The problems of HR in the financial sector

Since I became an independent consultant in 1993, the majority of my clients have been within financial services. As some common themes have emerged, I will discuss these as though I am describing one organisation.

The crucial challenge concerned organisational responsiveness to client needs: the intention being to build client and product knowledge across the organisation so as to enable the customisation of financial products. What was needed was a strong corporate culture for the markets that the organisation was servicing.

The issues being faced resulted from a particular phase of organisational development in which the emphasis had been placed on building strong individual business units. A drive for increased profitability had resulted in a divisional approach. As a result there was little sense of team cohesion across the organisation and a lack of group identity and corporate ethos. The organisation was also locked into a hierarchical career model with what has been described as a 'command and control' approach. This structure was clearly inhibiting decision-making, team-building and the flow of information across the organisation. The large number of corporate levels resulted in an internal emphasis, with effort concentrated on managing the relativities within a large corporate grouping. Such a predominantly inward-focused system meant that the HR processes lacked the sensitivity to the wider employment market. This would make them vulnerable to market pressures when economic recovery occurred.

The HR function had adopted a transaction-oriented approach to dealing with issues. While there was considerable HR activity, and many good initiatives, the overall human resources framework had not been defined. It was therefore questionable whether the HR activity was sufficiently focused or would assist the organisation in achieving its vision. In particular, the HR processes were not integrative – they did not help to bind the organisation together.

The challenge was not one of developing implementation strategies to help achieve synergy, creativity and responsiveness, but one of changing emotional mindsets and identifying vested power interests. Cultural change is a highly charged issue. One of the major hurdles in handling it is getting top management to understand that cultural development is, in fact, key. For some of my clients the word culture has been emotive; and for others the management of cultural diversity is a major headache. Yet the importance of developing the right culture for the organisation needs to be addressed and it should not be allowed to take place by default.

Strategies for success

Operational success in financial services is dependent on developing an environment which reflects the market-driven needs of its businesses to develop organisational agility. HR policies and procedures can facilitate this by being responsive to business needs and by creating a suitable environment for highly motivated and skilled individuals. I have already touched on cultural development, structural responsiveness and developing a proactive HR approach. When you are working inside an organisation, gaining commitment for implementation can be time-consuming because you are seen as being part of the system. As a consultant I have found consensus building is quicker. With an 'expert' label across the forehead you find that management is more receptive to new concepts and ideas. This is of particular value when some of the strategies cut across vested interests and power bases.

The areas that I have been working on as part of an overall

HR strategy can be grouped into three areas: cultivating a winning team; making an impact on the bottom line; and strengthening business partnership. Cultivating a winning team has, in many cases, involved cultural transition – from a role culture to a task/support culture. The tactics involved in this can mainly be classed as developmental; relating to top-team skills enhancement, team-building programmes with an emphasis on collaborative techniques, establishing effective communication channels and a structured training and development programme. Of these, the development programmes are key to the creation of a streamlined structure with fewer levels; the aim being to encourage co-operation and teamwork across the business.

To create a winning team, an organisation needs to acquire and retain highly motivated individuals who will have a direct impact on the bottom line. The major challenge in developing reward policies is that financial services have appeared largely to ignore all the studies on motivation and tended solely to use money as the prime motivator. The flaw in allowing the remuneration approach to performance management to be so dominant is that most organisations have to remain within a competitive market band to attract and retain their key people, irrespective of profitability. Given this, there is a strong case of moving towards a development-driven model of performance management which recognises intrinsic rewards, i.e. non-financial motivators. However, while in a number of organisations this approach is being explored, it is still considered to be money that motivates most of the people most of the time.

The third issue to consider is that of strengthening business partnership. Integration across the organisation needs to be encouraged at a number of levels. While initiatives to develop an open environment are crucial, there also needs to be recognition by the business that working in tandem with the HR function will bring added value and will be vital to the achievement of its vision. The role and contribution of the HR function in achieving this will be explored later.

The most difficult decision

The hardest decision that I had to make was whether to accept a downgraded role for the HR function in an effective merger of various corporate groupings or to stand up for my beliefs and take the consequences. My views on the role and contribution that HR should be making in an organisation are a leitmotif of this chapter. More importantly, they are passionately held.

During the 1980s the fortunes of many financial institutions fluctuated. It was an intensely competitive period as the investment banks became ruthlessly focused on gaining supremacy. County NatWest was no exception, although its tribulations became public news with the Blue Arrow affair. The life expectancy of CNW's management team was short. During my seven years there, there were five Chief Executives.

The role of HR in the financial sector is demanding and doubly so if you have to adapt and sell the function to a stream of new bosses. However the HR team demonstrated that it not only had the expertise but could contribute at a strategic level. This was recognised by the appointment of the head of the function as a member of the Management Committee. But it took five years of team development to ensure that a real impact could be made at all levels.

When CNW was wrapped up into a wider corporate grouping in NatWest Bank, the organisation chart showed that HR would have no direct reporting line to the new Chief Executive and would be encompassed in a support function. In fact, the HR department was bottom of the support functions listed. Those that have lived through a merger will appreciate the high level of emotional energy needed as various players jockey for key power positions. In common with a lot of mergers, taking time out to communicate, consult and to allay the fears of the workforce was not high on the agenda. The choice for me at the time was either to buy into a system where HR was seen as purely an administrative function or to leave in the company of a number of my senior colleagues. The outcome was inevitable.

Effective decision-making

The keys to effective decision-making are relatively simple. Taking the military model, these are to make a balanced appreciation of the situation; to assess and analyse all the factors involved; to explore all possible courses open; to focus on the solution to be adopted and then to come up with a coherent plan. Easy to define but often difficult to put into practice.

The reasons why decision-making is often flawed are due to a number of factors – most notably ego, the urge to control and fear of relinquishing power to others. But urgency also plays a part, as time-critical pressures mean that implementation becomes unstuck by not building consensus across a group and failing to take the time to understand individual needs and fears. And on a personal level, how many of us have not been sensitive to the 'inner-self'? Lost in a pile of paperwork, balancing too many conflicting priorities and hemmed in by peer group pressure we ignore the unease about a particular decision. In my experience these are always the decisions which come back to haunt you and demand further time and effort to resolve. On a grander scale, business decisions are often taken without considering the human element involved. The board often lacks a real insight into the only resource in an organisation which can sabotage its plans – the people.

The employee profile

We all recognise that the pace of change has intensified. Most business commentators point in the same direction and, in particular, the following trends have been identified: the need for large businesses to innovate; growing specialisation and internationalisation; flatter management structures; achievement through influence as opposed to command and control from an established power base; the growth in the employment of knowledge workers; demographic issues affecting the workforce mix; and, lastly, changing attitudes about working life.

There may well be differences of opinion about the exact pace of change, but it is clear that the organisation of the future will not operate on the basis that people will simply do what they are told. This has important implications for HR management. The precise skills and capabilities needed by the organisation will, of course, depend on the level at which recruiting is being undertaken. But regardless of this, we will need people who need to be challenged and who are flexible, receptive and enthusiastic about change.

If we consider recruitment at the level which will make that vital difference to the organisation in the future – management – we will need a core of individuals who are creative, innovative and who have lateral thinking ability. These talents need to be combined with teamworking and collaborative skills. Given that individuals are likely to be working in a flatter organisational structure, with emphasis being placed on establishing cross-disciplinary teams and developing lateral relationships, better interpersonal skills will also be needed, in particular influencing ones. In general, we will be seeking people with good HR skills: as the workforce becomes more sophisticated and demanding, we will need managers who understand something about organisational behaviour and who demonstrate a greater degree of subtlety and sensitivity in their management of people. Future managers will need to have a real feel for the human issues.

While we can identify what we expect from those we employ, more will be demanded from us as employers. Certainly we cannot continue to adopt the 'cookie cutter' approach to recruitment – everyone in the same mould. We are going to have to rethink organisational life to make it more attractive to a wider group of individuals. This will require a far more flexible approach to those who are balancing work and family pressures and who do not wish to be workaholics. There is still resistance towards women and minority groups. We have to recognise that for a large section of the workforce the glass ceiling is triple glazed. The organisation will have to focus on the development of general HR skills and techniques within a wider group as well as on top-team development, team-building and cultural awareness programmes. We may even have to consider making work a lot more fun.

Does Personnel have a role in the boardroom?

A boardroom without a strong HR presence is seriously deficient. The strategic direction of the business involves having skilled people in the right jobs. It is the creative talent of these people which determines whether the business will be successful or not. Organisational capability depends on creating a culture which maximises the potential of employees to meet new business challenges. HR has a key role in the cultural development of the organisation. It is this area which has a direct impact on strategy.

HR has to be at the top of a boardroom's agenda. It is the HR function which is the steward of the institution's most important asset, and therefore it must have a place within the top team. Strategy involves people to a greater or lesser extent. People need new skills to meet business challenges, the management succession of the business is people driven, and it is people who will build and shape the future direction of the business.

The board should therefore be concerned with what is needed to attract people to the organisation and how they are developed, trained, rewarded and motivated. In order to do this, it should be ensuring that the organisation's HR policies and procedures underpin the business strategy. The board will need an HR director who has the capability and determination to contribute at a strategic level and is an active member of the management team. We, as HR professionals, must demonstrate our ability at this level and make that vital difference.

Personnel and today's key business challenges?

Once upon a time there were staff, then personnel, and now we have human resources. Many professionals feel that this reclassification is purely cosmetic – others that it reflects the changes organisations have made to confront a dramatically changing business environment. Many of us would agree that the relationship between line management, employees and HR professionals has altered.

Most of us would now accept that line management must take more responsibility for HR management issues. This trend was identified in the Price Waterhouse/Cranfield project on international strategic human resource management, particularly the devolution of training and development to line management. Given the pace of change, new skills will be required of both line management and the HR function. One view is that HR will shift to a more strategic advisory role. The HR function will therefore act in partnership with line management in shaping the strategic direction of the business. How this will happen and what constitutes best practice is being explored. We have to ask ourselves the question: is there a strategic domain for HR?

If this strategic domain is emerging we need to consider what HR strategy actually consists of: is it (a) an after the event analysis of business strategy; (b) an integral part of business strategy (the textbook answer); or (c) a separate stand-alone input to business strategy? Martyn Sloman (Head of Training and Development at NatWest Markets) and I would suggest that it is the third option. For those of you who agree, the hopes, ambitions, perceptions and motivation of the workforce will be the strategic domain of the HR professional.

The next question to ask ourselves is: does HR have the ability to deliver? Let's assume we have extended our skills base in areas such as selling, influencing, consultancy and networking. In other words we have acquired the necessary professional capability. We then need to focus on developing a business-driven approach. HR policies have to underpin the strategy of the business. With the quickening pace of change, successful organisations will be those that actively manage the process of change. It is here that HR has a pivotal role to play.

However, in many organisations personnel people are still seen as business preventers. Personnel processes have become an end in themselves; they are used to control not to facilitate. In rejecting this role the new HR department has to accept that the line must take on more responsibility for day-to-day personnel activities. Line managers, in turn, must develop new skills in HR management and accept a dynamic role for the HR function. The HR function, of course, has to ensure that it has the necessary specialist expertise in core HR areas, e.g. reward management, incentivisation, recruitment and selection, per-formance appraisal, etc.; but above all it has to ensure that it has the capability and *determination* to contribute to the strategic development of the business. It should be creating a proactive and constructive partnership with line management. We have to recognise that the role of personnel has changed. We can no longer hide behind the HR manual which has been used as a source of power. We should not be frightened by this change but see it as a challenge to create a new role as a facilitator, adviser and strategist, and above all else as an active member of the management team.

This role will involve developing the capability of the business to attract and motivate high-calibre staff, in order to facilitate the seizing of business opportunities. The new HR function should be concerned about the education and training of line management in HR issues, the control of the quality of the HR function once it is devolved to the line, and the strategic management of this relationship. Our role will be about understanding the capability of the organisation, examining the areas where it is not performing and the reasons why, and creating solutions to ensure that it has the capacity to meet its business objectives and the challenges it will face in the future.

The years ahead

The main challenge within financial services will be the management of human resources. It will be this that creates the competitive edge. Many organisations blinded by the recession are failing even to put the cornerstones in place to address this challenge. There is an assumption that there will always be a pool of skilled labour available which can be managed with the same set of skills as before.

As regards meeting organisational challenges, Professor Andrew Kakabadse of Cranfield argues that a vision for the future will have long-term viability only if it is shared by the top team. It is essential that this team creates an open atmosphere and offers and receives mutual feedback. Yet many would ask whether financial services has any real managers. Top teams often include a high proportion of individuals who are purely product or transaction orientated – the deal junkies. Their vision is often myopic, they tend to be prima donnas by temperament and part of a culture which complains. Creating top team capability is one of the main issues facing the financial sector. That core of individuals with breadth, vision and the necessary leadership skills to drive the business forward is a rare commodity.

Consensus in the top team will be tested by the management of cultural diversity. This is one of the critical issues facing this sector. I have grouped the management of cultural diversity under the headings of: the Born to be a Bureaucrat Syndrome, the Continental European Dilemma, and Managing the Specialist.

The Born to be a Bureaucrat Syndrome particularly afflicts retail banks. This sector tends to have well-defined systems, rigid hierarchies and established structures. Their personnel processes are geared to control careers 'from the cradle to the grave'. The 'lifers' attitude breeds an institutional mindset where flexibility is not part of the vocabulary, procedural considerations are paramount and information gets sucked into a black hole of analysis/paralysis, compounded by endless working parties.

Most people who are clients of a retail bank have stories of an acute lack of customer focus. There is little understanding of what customers want, why they want it and how much they are prepared to pay for added value. This is not principally a question of the quality of staff but of their operational framework. For example, at Coutts & Co you will meet staff with similar skills, background and educational qualifications to those in the typical retail bank. However, these people will not have been forced to swallow the procedural pill – the manual – but are working in a culture which deals with the customer as an individual rather than as an item to be processed.

In striving to gain control of costs and in implementing the subsequent downsizing exercises, the retail banks have torpedoed their culture. This was a culture based on the equation of loyalty and career security. They are now grappling with the question of what sort of culture to create. It will not be good enough merely to inform employees that they now only offer jobs not careers. The challenge they are facing is to turn an inward-looking, home-grown system outwards to become client focused. In order to do this, they will have to acquire the managerial skills to respond to a fast and fluid environment and create flexible structures which can deal with pace of change.

The Continental European Dilemma is interesting to observe. The challenges facing the retail banks are similar to those faced by the heavy-weight continental institutions who have been buying into an Anglo-Saxon business culture. They desire creative corporate finance, the enthusiasm of young people fresh off the leash, the experience of aggressive/hostile takeover skills (unknown in Central Europe) and the sharp focus of London and New York negotiating teams. Their aim is admirable, but the execution more complex. There is a cultural divide between the entrepreneurs and the monolith of apparatchiks. The German and Swiss Supervisory Boards know what they are doing and their vision and strategy is well-defined; but the layers of functionaries beneath may not understand that strategy. Execution is severely prejudiced by the system which cannot accommodate unorthodox flair, rapid decision-making, passion and autonomy.

Cultural challenges also face the Japanese and Americans, but regardless of cultural roots all financial organisations will face the dilemma of managing the small specialist group: teams with high intellect, specialist talent, motivated and in demand, but wanting a direct share of their contribution. These teams have far less interest in the employer than in their own employability. They will seek to ply their trade with the institution who creates the best opportunity for them to succeed – the one which has the best reputational umbrella, credit rating and muscle under which to shelter. This will not be a passive employer/employee relationship but one which will need to be dynamically managed and nurtured.

There is an arrogance in financial services about its own ability to manage people. Yet the sector has not excelled itself in cultural understanding. During the run up to the 'Big Bang' and its aftermath, disastrous mistakes were made in acquiring and merging different skill bases. The management of the 1980s adopted a short-term approach, treating individuals like a commodity to trade. Today there is still a lack of quality HR skills. Below the surface of many firms bubbles a real discontent, because people have been treated with a cavalier attitude. This discontent will prove disastrous once the employment market becomes buoyant. Yet a major gap can be identified between talking about HR as the most valuable asset and translating this into action. A major hurdle is the lack of top team understanding of the HR challenges presented by this decade.

An illustration of this occurred when I was discussing the role of HR with senior people at a major financial institution. One person stated that he wished the HR function to become proactive. His definition of being proactive was for the function to write a new maternity leave policy. When informed that the HR department should be in partnership with line management, one of his colleagues retorted 'Do you see yourself as an equal or working for us?'

These dynamics will create a powerful opportunity for human resource professionals in financial services. Those that are administrators by inclination will flounder. The successful ones, however, will challenge the organisation to raise the level of capability and to create an environment in which this can be achieved.

References

1 This was described in RILEY, Kathryn and SLOMAN, Martyn 'Milestones for the Personnel Department', *Personnel Management*, August 1991.

 # The Line Management Perspective

Ewart Wooldridge

An irresistible theme

The theme of 'A View from the Bridge' is very appealing. On those rare occasions I can escape from the challenges of the South Bank Centre, I take to the water (though not to the Thames). I have to admit that my vessel has no bridge. I travel under sail, usually taking a circuitous route that involves endless tacking, gybing and going about – perhaps familiar characteristics of the daily life of the typical human resources professional!

I am also attracted to the theme because it implies a key role in *steering* the ship – not necessarily the experience of most personnel professionals if they are honest with themselves. In my case, addressing this theme comes at the same time as taking on a *line* director role – and discovering just how much wider a view I have from the bridge with the line management perspective. I will be returning many times to this crucial issue of the line/personnel relationship. It seems vital, at this time, for new and challenging things to be said about the line/ personnel interface if the personnel profession is to retain anything approaching a 'leading edge'. (By the way, I start from the pessimistic assumption that the 'profession' of personnel or human resource management may well have reached and passed its zenith and be on a gradual – though not irreversible – descent. This is particularly so if it cannot define the HRM/line management relationship in a more exciting and 'value-added' way.)

The really irresistible ingredient in the nautical theme is the concept of a *journey*. Looking back to where we have come from is as important as looking at where we are now – and both contribute to shaping the vision of where we are sailing in the future. With these multiple perspectives, I will start my journey – pausing from time to time to summarise the sign-posts, or marker buoys. Let me start with a bit of retrospection and introspection, by probing the depths of my own HR philosophy.

Industrial relations is dead: long live employee relations!

Industrial relations is now so out of fashion, you dare not admit even to your closest friends that it was once a key part of your career. If you do admit it, they immediately assume that you were responsible for the malevolent conspiracy that brought us the three-day week, Arthur Scargill and the demise of most of the British manufacturing sector. If you admit it to modern HR professionals, you are immediately stamped as the old-guard 'smoke-filled room' merchants.

I openly admit to being a graduate of the industrial relations school of personnel, entering the profession in 1969 at the same time as the ink was drying on the Donovan Commission Report into British industrial relations and Barbara Castle's *In Place of Strife* was collapsing about her.

I actually committed the even greater sin of joining the Engineering Employers' Federation, the institution which – it was alleged – Donovan was set up to attack. And if there was ever a fruitless journey (by rail, not sea), it was the trip to York for the national stage of the industry's disputes procedure, operated by the EEF. Issues travelled relentlessly up from Works Conference to Local Conference, and thence to Central Conference at the Royal Station Hotel at York – only to be referred back down to Local or Works Conference level without resolution, for further discussion, and then possibly to be referred back to York . . . and so on . . . . It was a magnificent ritual – a 'total experience' rather than a mere disputes procedure. And whilst virtually every *formal* dispute that was referred up was never resolved, the bars of the Royal Station Hotel were the venue for the resolution of all the other disputes which never found their way into the procedure in the first place.

That era is thankfully dead, as is the industrial relations tradition which spawned sham (or simply ineffective) productivity agreements, automatic indexing of pay deals or fiddling one's way through Government pay policies. Two particularly bad but amusing experiences of my own in that crazy IR world spring to mind. The first is of an infamous London Branch Secretary of a well-known printing union who told me of his pride at having conned a Fleet Street Personnel Director into drawing up a productivity deal which had amongst its beneficiaries seven deceased members. The second was the ITV company which was talked into conceding a special allowance to its *sound* engineers for the introduction of *colour* television: think about it!

These bad practices and agreements may be long buried or reversed, but those personnel professionals who were able to achieve genuine and lasting change against this appalling backcloth used a quite astonishing repertoire of management and negotiating skills in the process – skills that perhaps are scorned today and may be in increasingly short supply. As I stand on this mythical bridge, I see a number of key issues arising from this analysis.

Firstly, we should be quite assertive that the skills and insights associated with employee relations (to use a more acceptable term for IR) are not redundant. They are vital amongst the core skills of the HR or line manager simply because they so often play a key part in the management of change. This has nothing to do with whether the workforce is unionised or not – nor with its size. It is simply a recognition that any group of individuals thrown together in a work environment will act and react in a multiplicity of ways – as individuals, as departments, as teams and as a total mass. The skills and sensitivities involved in 'reading', interpreting and predicting the feelings of those different groupings should still be at the core of an HR practitioner's repertoire. The combined effect of recession, employment law and the declining power of the unions in recent years has encouraged an arrogant and lazy assumption that most kinds of change can be driven through and any resistance which might be put up can be demolished. Yet too often I have seen senior management assumptions about 'shoving change through' which end up snatching defeat out of the jaws of victory. So often, the service that the Chief Executive wants from the personnel professional is the answer to the question: 'how will the workforce react?' The ability to answer this question accurately and perceptively is one of the key factors that keeps the HR professional in the driving seat of the effective management of change, demonstrably adding value, and therefore in demand from line managers.

Secondly, I believe that the ability to negotiate within an organisation is quite simply one of life's core skills. This has nothing to do with trade unions or collective bargaining, although for many it may have been acquired in that arena, and for some it may have to continue to be practised in that setting if we are to accept Sid Kessler's[1] robust reaffirmation of the values of trade union recognition and collective bargaining. It is, first and foremost, a skill essential to the scenario of modern organisations in which networking lies at the heart of successful management, where supply chains have replaced vertically integrated systems, and where positive outcomes in negotiations over roles or supply relationships can be crucial to commercial success. Sadly, I come across too many HR professionals for whom negotiation is a dirty word – or it is something that produces severe anxiety symptoms in them.

Coaching line managers in the art of negotiation – in the widest sense of the word – should be a key priority for HR practitioners. Two particular training experiences I went through provided me with concepts which I still practice today. The first was 'controlled pace negotiation'. This taught me the skills of negotiation literally in slow motion. It instilled in me the importance of thorough analysis and preparation, the importance of good listening skills to understand the other party's position properly, and the confidence to pace the process and control its speed. The other training was in 'influencing skills'. This demonstrated the simple point that negotiation was usually more about the interpersonal behaviours which went on *between* the formal negotiations and which thereby created the scenario for agreement. There are too many managers going around proud of their reputation of being Attila the Hun – and too many who are still not aware that they have that reputation.

Thirdly, a good experience of employee relations teaches you that protocol counts. This is nothing to do with boring and bureaucratic consultation procedures. People at work expect to be treated with respect and dignity. However fast and continuous the pace of change, people still need to be listened to and involved, and the pay-off to management is enormous. Even during the sad and negative process of running down TVS and declaring most of its workforce redundant, although I could have got away with the most ruthless approach, I made time to involve staff and the return was immense in terms of the bottom line, and the maintenance of quality and morale to the end.

Summary

- Whilst rejecting the 'unacceptable face' of IR, we should recognise that dealing with relationships in the workplace still lies at the heart of people management.
- Negotiation, influencing skills and the ability to 'read' the collective feelings of the workforce are core skills which add real value to the effectiveness of the HR practitioner.
- In its quest for the purity of HRM, Personnel should be careful not to play down these vital skills.

Creativity, innovation and organisational change

With nearly 14 years' experience of working in the creative, media and arts sectors, it is not surprising that I am passionately committed to the processes of fostering a culture of creativity and innovation. It was hugely exciting to be part of the team at Granada which created *Brideshead Revisited* and *The Jewel in the Crown* and to witness the processes that held together that award-winning, world-beating team. At the South Bank, we are the largest arts complex in Europe, if not in the world; and in the arts, as in the media, we as a nation are still, quite rightly, regarded as world leaders in quality. Creativity and innovation naturally lie at the heart of the success of UK plc in all its sectors – not just the 'artistic' – yet there are too many examples of how we have had the lead snatched away from us. As the ability of our own workforce to innovate is increasingly the key to maintaining a leading edge and differentiating ourselves from our competitors, we should bring this issue to the top of the people agenda. The IPM is particularly well placed to take a leading role, as the Institute is at the centre of the debate about people, organisations and their development. Most importantly, any study of the issue should look as much at what has been happening to organisational change as much as looking at the individual and creativity.

Few texts have summarised the creative process better for me than the section on innovation in *Thriving on Chaos*,[2] and I promise the reader this will be my only quotation from Tom Peters. Apart from his alluring concept of 'creative swiping' (not to be confused with pure copying!), he concentrates on a number of key issues. Uniqueness and innovation rarely come from one breakthrough idea achieved through individual analysis. He talks about uniqueness most often 'coming from the accumulation of thousands of tiny enhancements'. It is as much a synthesizing process as an analytical one. It is about talented people working together in teams, in the right physical environment, and in the right proximity to one another. It is

about creating an environment in which dedication to innovation thrives and failure is tolerated.

Let us now contrast this model with what has been happening in organisations in recent years, and in particular to the
highly seductive influences of Charles Handy's[3] models of
organisations and developments in 'internal markets'. (Space
considerations do not permit me to give a detailed summary of
his concepts, but if I list such items as 'shamrock organisations', 'core staff v. periphery', 'outsourcing', and the 'flexible
organisation', I hope most readers will know what I am talking
about.)

Commercial television provided a useful testing ground for
the implementation of these ideas in the late-1980s, as we
moved from contracting out the obvious peripheral services
(catering, security, cleaning, site maintenance, installation
work and other support activities) to a situation where at least
25 per cent of the core production work was outsourced as
well. From there it did not require a major leap to encourage
the notion of the 'publisher contractor' which put out to
contract most or all of its production. And there was, of
course, the successful model of Channel 4 to emulate. Now we
are witnessing the fascinating stresses inside the BBC with the
implementation of Producer Choice, where every programme
maker is a 'buyer' and every resource department a 'seller' of
resources.

I have no intention of joining the debate about Producer
Choice, nor for that matter about internal markets in the
health service or education. However, what my experience
tells me – and the Tom Peters model confirms – is that talent
thrives in 'critical masses', and that as we pursue the outsourcing model, we must be sure that we have somehow left
intact – or held together somewhere else under the organisation's control – the protective framework that allows talent,
innovation and creativity to be nurtured and supported.

The flexible organisation provides a lot of new challenges
and opportunities for the human resource professional. First,
HR managers should be providing a major input into such

organisational choices – after all, it is a key part of their expertise. Secondly, they should be vigilant in seeking to protect those parts of the organisation whose creativity and innovation are crucial to survival and growth. Thirdly, as organisational change continues to develop around it, the HR function itself may face its own challenges as it contemplates whether it is a critical mass of talent to be protected or a seller of services that can function more effectively at the contracted-out fringe.

Summary

- Innovation and creativity are the lifeblood of most organisations; let's bring them higher on the HR agenda.
- The shamrock organisation, outsourcing and internal markets are producing fundamental changes in organisational flexibility; what are they doing to creativity, innovation and the nurturing of talent?
- What's happening to quality and innovation in HR departments with these new organisational structures? Are they an opportunity or a threat?

Leadership and Communication – controlling the medium and the message

Thank goodness leadership is back in fashion as a management concept. I suppose it went out of fashion for two reasons. First, and maybe unfairly, it became associated with somewhat rigid, mechanistic theories which seemed to draw too heavily upon armed forces concepts. Secondly, leadership became a more complex issue to define when, thanks to union power, the pluralist ideology was in the ascendant. As the late 1980s and early '90s have allowed the unitary framework fully to assert itself (though not for ever, perhaps), we can revisit the question of leadership with some confidence. I was very pleased to see the Industrial Society publishing a fascinating set of case studies in 1992 under the title: *Leaders: The learning curve of achievement.*[4] For me, the subject allows me to explore two crucial components of leadership which must never slip down the HR agenda: communication and the setting of values.

Poor communications still so often seem to be one of the root causes when things go wrong. When I was working in engineering, we did some fascinating research into how senior executives of engineering companies came across in their own company newspapers and into the readability of these crucial vehicles of their written communications strategy. Many of these executives received some very nasty shocks when we held the mirror up in front of them. Their image in the eyes of their staff was overwhelmingly affected by how they appeared in the photographs and what they were doing in them. Since the majority of photographs were often of presentations, retirements and other official social gatherings where a glass of wine was naturally in hand, they quite incorrectly conveyed the impression of a largely socialising existence normally under the influence of alcohol.

The picture did not get much better when we looked at readability. We developed two standard measures, based on sentence and word length and on the ratio of white space to print, which allowed comparisons to be made with types of national newspapers. Invariably these official organs tended to veer wildly from the appearance of *The Sun* (when times were good) to the *Financial Times* (when the news was bad) – ranging from the insulting to the incomprehensible. Qualitative judgements on the content and style were also often not very sympathetic. 'Could do better' was the report we had to give in many cases, or at least 'could be more sensitive'.

Chief Executives are also keen advocates of 'team briefing' or 'briefing groups', captivated by the thought that their carefully chosen phrases will inspire the staff as the message cascades through the organisation like an effervescent mountain stream. There is no doubt that some fine examples of briefing group systems exist – but they are so vulnerable to failure as the stream of ideas either dries up or becomes perceived as a torrent of propaganda. I have to admit that we encountered this latter problem at TVS when we hit serious trading difficulties, and once the damage is done it is difficult to restore confidence and trust in the system. Such briefing systems also require a very high level of routine maintenance, particularly to ensure that the briefers down the line have the skill to translate the message from the top into the appropriate language of their own briefing group.

My experience of the successful management of change suggests that there is no satisfactory substitute for regular communication on a direct face-to-face basis, however time-consuming that is for Chief Executives and other senior managers. Only this method conveys the true determination which is going to win over hearts and minds. In the Industrial Society's book, *Leaders: The learning curve of achievement*,[5] the authors report on Sir Graham Day's comment that, when he was trying to turn round Cammell Laird, 'I talked till hell froze over'. Dr. Brian Smith, describing his battle with Elders for Control of Metal Box, maintained: 'You had to go out and persuade people; people will understand all the logic, but in the end, they are only convinced by passion and the belief you bring.'

At TVS, because we had the technology readily available, we became very successful at conducting live interactive broadcasts that enabled the Chief Executive and the rest of his senior management team to achieve a high level of direct 'face-to-face' communication simultaneously with a lot of staff in a multi-site organisation. As telephone and television technology become increasingly integrated, and this approach becomes more readily available, HRM practitioners should be ready to meet the very real training and coaching needs that this style of communication creates. And they should generally be more vigilant in watching over the quality of other communication media: how interesting are the messages on video monitors (or are they just perceived as another form of propaganda in a modern format?); how tidy and up-to-date are the noticeboards; how relevant are the management structure charts – do they display yesterday's team? Do they even display the right photograph against each name or job title?

Whilst we must rightly be obsessed with the medium, what about the quality of the message? As I stand on the bridge of this metaphorical ship, I see a lot of bottles washed up on the beach of a nearby island, containing messages that no one's bothered to read. These are called 'Mission Statements'. Probably some of the most boring and unreadable pieces of writing are to be found in the form of mission or vision statements. And they are supposed to be inspirational! I always follow Charles Handy's maxim that the vision 'should create the "Aha Effect" . . . as when everyone says "Aha, of course, now I see it", like wit perhaps – what often was thought but ne'er so well expressed'.[6] I particularly like his reference to humour, because it is the mechanisms within humour which give the reader or listener a jolt, and open up a sudden new perspective they did not expect to see. When I was in TVS, we used the mechanisms of humour in a number of our training interventions. As a student of French, I commend all of you who would like to pursue this idea to read *Le Rire* (*Laughter*) by Henri Bergson, and then plan your training accordingly!

There is only one thing worse than a Mission Statement that is boring, and that is one which is well understood but at odds with the values and standards actually practised by key representatives of the organisation. I believe that Chief Executives underestimate the extent to which this can be a major factor influencing the moral and motivation of the workforce. As we make great strides to establish increasingly unitary organisations and direct and visible leadership from the front, so we have exposed to closer inspection the quality of that leadership. There are no right or absolute answers to the complex questions of directors' remuneration or the tax affairs of the Director General of a major public corporation. However all these matters have to be dealt with and communicated in a fashion that will not get in the way of the organisation objectives, particularly if the organisation's is in the middle of a major change programme which requires the enthusiastic commitment of the workforce as a whole.

The preservation of the proper standards and values of the organisation has traditionally been associated with the personnel function, although usually focused almost exclusively upon equal opportunities policies. I firmly believe that for the really effective personnel practitioner, the values brief must go wider than that. Employees are increasingly influenced by what the organisation stands for and are more sensitive to any mismatch between what senior executives say and what they do. As there is less scope for the traditional wage/work contract, the psychological contract assumes a greater significance. Such a psychological contract may be concerned with development of the individual in the context of the 'learning organisation', it may be affected by the remuneration of board members; it may equally be heavily influenced by issues of fairness, in an equal opportunities sense or otherwise. Whatever it is, the HR function must be vigilant in patrolling these frontiers of perceived fairness, particularly as the workforce becomes more dominated by 'knowledge workers' with higher and more sophisticated expectations of company standards.

Summary

- Leadership is not seen frequently enough on the HR agenda.
- Communication is central to the skills of leadership – we must revisit the traditional methods and provide strong guidance and training on putting new communications technology to its fullest use.
- Personnel should not just be the custodian of statutory values such as equal opportunities but also of the values

which underpin the legitimacy of leadership within the organisation.

Implementing change and maintaining the momentum

My preoccupation over the last few years can be summed up in two words – 'managing change'. Whether it has taken the form of TQM, quality circles, performance management, transformation of working practices or just plain redundancy, it has invariably been expressed as a 'programme of change' and has represented a concentrated burst of organisational energy with management in the driving seat. It was often painful and stressful, but also exhilarating. However, for many of us, I would suggest that we found the exercise easier than we thought. This was because there was an overwhelming reason for change arising from the surrounding economic context, and a workforce (and unions, where they existed) which had little ability to fight back.

What surprises me, even today, is the general assumption amongst the majority of employees that ongoing change is undesirable. Although there are many spectacular exceptions, I suspect that the concept of 'kaizen', or continuous change and improvement, is a long way off in most organisations. We can achieve 'step change' once, maybe twice, but we soon encounter a kind of change fatigue. In the many years that I have been practising and studying the management of change, I have been most fascinated to uncover the roots of resistance to change and from that to identify the factors that foster a 'climate of change'. Three common factors seem to be associated with resistance to change and hence offer the key to creating that positive climate:

- lack of common understanding about change *within the management team*;
- poor awareness by managers of the attitudes and feelings of the workforce;

- a sense of defeatism that it just cannot be done and is too difficult.

The first of these is of overwhelming importance and goes right to the top of the organisation. How often have I seen a schism in the senior management team wreak more havoc with a change programme than any organised resistance from the trade unions. The need for a clear and common sense of direction right through the management team is a prerequisite of success – and, as I indicated earlier, that does not just mean a fancy 'mission statement' but a genuine sense of team cohesiveness that infects the rest of the management team.

The second of these factors relates to the lack of employee relations sensitivity on the part of managers at all levels. They need to be able to empathise with the workforce – to read their collective minds in the way I described at the beginning of this chapter. Those that have this ability often belong to the MBWA school of management – that is, 'management by walking about'.

The third one – the sense of defeatism – may also sadly have its roots in management attitudes and has to be continuously worked on by coaching, counselling and development. It may well be stress related, and I have found that the use of stress workshops are a critical prelude to a change programme. Powerful leadership skills from the top, as I described earlier, may play a crucial part in overcoming the sense of defeatism. As John Harvey-Jones wrote in *Making It Happen*: 'The task of leadership is really to make the status quo more dangerous than launching into the unknown.'[7]

The real challenge therefore is not just the management of change as a one-off exercise, but *maintaining the momentum* in periods when the overwhelming case for change may have temporarily gone into abeyance. The post-recession personnel managers must be right at the heart of the process of making this happen. In Michael Armstrong's words, they should be there 'as facilitators, catalysts, enablers, change agents and creators of environments conducive to successful accomplishment.'[8]

Summary

- A crucial attribute of successful managers is their ability to induce change.
- Only by offering that service too – whether from an HRM, employee relations or development role – can personnel practitioners hope to retain a leading edge role in most organisations.
- The real challenge from now on is to use those abilities to create a climate of continuous change in organisations.

So where does Personnel go from here?

I have deliberately presented an image of Personnel strongly biased towards a proactive and dynamic role in the organisation. Michael Armstrong in *Personnel and the Bottom Line* said: 'There is always a danger in personnel management, if it is perceived mainly as an administrative function, of it spending too much time making inefficient organisations efficient'.[9] Often, to its credit, it does that exceptionally well! But even the scope for doing those administrative functions may be diminishing as IT systems offer the opportunity to line managers to hold their own personnel database, and finance departments to do the salary administration. Even in the crucial area of resourcing, my experience is that recruitment and manpower planning are no longer as central to personnel as they were. These are increasingly a line responsibility. As I look out for the last time from my bridge, the crucial issues which I see are:

- effective relations in the workplace;

- creativity and innovation;
- getting the best out of new organisation structures;
- credible and forceful leadership; and
- maintaining a climate of continuous willingness to change.

All these are close to the heart of the business, are about adding value, and all require a high level of people management skills. However, as I view this from a line management perspective, these skills are, more than ever before, embedded in a partnership between line and personnel. I inevitably see an 'open systems' concept of personnel with training methodologies and qualifications which appeal to a wide cross-section of management whilst still allowing for the maintenance of a framework of professional discipline. This may sound a contradiction, but in reality it is not one if we accept that HRM is central to the practice of good management, and that the Institute has a unique role – from the basis of carefully defined standards of professional competence – to exert a major influence on the general level of management thinking and behaviour across all sectors of the UK economy.

References

1 KESSLER, Sid. 'Is there still a future for the unions?' *Personnel Management*, July 1993.
2 PETERS, Tom. *Thriving on Chaos*. Macmillan, 1987.
3 HANDY, Charles. *The Age of Unreason*. Hutchinson, 1989.
4 FORREST and TOLFREE. *Leaders: The learning curve of achievement*. Industrial Society Press, 1992.
5 *ibid.*
6 HANDY, Charles. *op. cit.*
7 HARVEY-JONES, John. *Making it Happen*. Fontana, 1988.
8 ARMSTRONG, Michael. *Personnel and the Bottom Line*. IPM, 1986.
9 *ibid.*

 The Power of Vision

Stephen Connock

At first glance, the role of the HR Manager in the mid-1990s would appear to be secure. After all, HR Managers are engaged in most of the major drivers to organisational success. Performance management, culture change programmes, empowerment schemes, reward strategies, communications and other subjects fill the agenda. Yet doubts remain. One of the questions to be addressed in this book is: does Personnel have a role in the boardroom? To me it is surprising the question has to be asked, yet I am sure the IPM do not mean to be merely rhetorical in shaping this question. Of course, no one doubts the importance of people in generating corporate success, especially in the context of the increasing importance of the individual's knowledge and skills as sources of competitive advantage. No, the doubt seems to be about the HR function itself, not the subject matter. Why? There are tensions and ambiguities in the role, to be sure.[1] Are we there to counsel or control, to advise or decide? Today, most HR Managers would emphasise their coaching role; indeed, some job titles are changing from HR Manager to HR Consultant to strengthen the point. However, internal cost pressures still create the necessity for HR Managers to act in control mode, although increasingly – and rightly – such controls are vested in senior line management.

So, tensions remain. Doubts about the function also reflect concerns about the competencies of the individuals concerned, especially about the business skills and knowledge of the HR Manager. Financial competency is – shall I say – not as well developed as it might be. There has perhaps (again I express it delicately) been an over-concern with the development of the individual in isolation from the business context. Highly trained and developed staff whose roles do not, nor may ever,

141

require their new skills to be applied cannot be justified in business terms. In more generous years, such social engineering would have been valuable in itself. In the context of a recession, with gross margins under severe pressure, with headcount reduction continuing especially in indirect areas, with competition heightening, the HR activities must contribute directly and unambiguously to business priorities.

HR philosophy

These introductory remarks will provide many clues to my underlying HR philosophy. HR management, and the HR function, must be aligned to the organisation's mission, and support the achievement of strategic objectives. The 'fit' needs to be close in both philosophy and actions. Lack of 'fit' will result sooner or later in an adverse organisational response – for example, changing the reporting line of the HR Manager, replacing the HR Manager or simply marginalising the function and the people within it. A telling early symptom of lack of 'fit' is the expression of doubts about the role of HR in the business. These dangers can be avoided. To do so requires attention to fundamentals, including:

- developing an HR vision;
- introducing clear performance measures;
- maintaining high standards of professionalism and quality.

Developing an HR vision

The power of vision must not be underestimated. Arising from, and reinforcing, the organisation's mission, the HR vision should seek to define what you and line management want to achieve in HR terms, and what you and line management want the function to be, and do, to support these goals. The HR vision needs to be:

- cohesive – providing a common thread linking the business mission with subsequent HR strategies;
- long-term – setting the future agenda;
- inspiring – providing motivation through the reinstatement of core values;
- energising – creating greater certainty of HR aims and a unifying sense of direction throughout the organisation;
- focused – giving all staff, and the HR function in particular, clarity of purpose;
- measurable – providing a yardstick to judge future performance.

So, my philosophy starts with the power of vision: know what you want to achieve; know your underlying values; reinforce the business mission.[2]

The HR vision can be developed by reviewing trends around key issues, or clusters. Table 1 shows in summary form a typical 'cluster analysis'. Here the trend over time can be analysed, drawing out in the future section the elements of the HR vision. Table 1 identifies the 'network organisation', openness, empowerment, peer appraisal and IT as key future drivers. I return to these themes below in more detail.

Table 1

Developing an HR Vision

Clusters	Past	Now	Future
• Organisation	Centralised and functional	Devolved to business units	Network organisation
• Style	Paternalistic	Participative	Open and empowered
• Processes	Self-appraisal	Management appraisal	Peer appraisal
• Competencies	Low IT	IT awareness	IT competency at all levels

Performance measures

Secondly, I emphasise performance measures. Readers persuaded of the importance of a clear long-term direction may find a concentration on measurement too narrow, even dangerous. After all (if I may paraphrase Gresham) may not bad measures drive out good judgements? I accept care is needed in the measurement field. Ratios can over-simplify the position; the measurement can become too complex, leading to 'analysis paralysis'; we may forget that measures are a means to an end, not an end in themselves. And yet, HR measurement can allow the HR Manager to demonstrate the achievement of goals compared historically within the business or against external benchmarks.

Effective HR measurement should be simple (relying on up to 10 basic indices), should be widely communicated and should track progress over time, deriving from baseline data. You need to be asking yourself: 'where do I want to be in five years' time?' as regards a range of key performance indicators, including training spend per capita, headcount by function/ business, HR costs in relation to total costs, and so on. Again, the indices you choose will relate to the goals identified in the HR vision. Intermediate performance milestones can be defined to judge progress. Regular monitoring will reveal problem areas, and suggest actions to realign progress towards the vision.

Professionalism and quality

Finally, I emphasised professionalism. To me, this means delivering objectives to high standards at all times. Much of the underlying philosophy of Total Quality can be repeated here with complete conviction: right first time, every time; continuously seeking to learn and improve; working to the highest possible standards. Adherence to such personal concepts can quickly spread to others, creating for the function a sense of momentum, action centredness, a 'can do' style and service

orientation which will add to overall credibility and effectiveness.

Greatest problems, and coping strategies

My current and recent problem areas have to do with managing change in large and complex organisations. More specifi-
cally, how do you achieve commitment to and motivation
about the vision and strategic objectives at all levels in the
organisation? Senior managers (hopefully) feel a strong sense
of shared commitment to the organisation's goals, yet something generally goes wrong in the middle of the hierarchy.
Instead of commitment, there is at best tacit agreement, at
worst covert resistance. Further down the line there is cynicism. Have they not seen it all before? Initiatives seem to come
and go: why should the latest 'big idea' be any different?[3]

These are deep issues, which touch on values, style, power,
culture. Such resistance is more likely in a downsizing context.
Rosabeth Moss Kantor[4] addressed the characteristics required
of the 'change agent' confronted by these obstacles. These
included:

- providing clarity of direction;
- participating – encouraging others to be part of the team;
- persuading and being persistent;
- repeatedly demonstrating your own commitment to the
  change;
- looking for early successes to serve as models and rewarding 'exemplars';
- creating a sense of excitement about the future.

These are important pointers to success in the management
of change. However, an underlying issue remains: why do
people not participate? Clearly there are some personality

issues here – some people do not need or want influence (thank goodness). In my experience, staff generally want to be involved, and have the skills to contribute. The challenge is to harness such energy to the organisation's ends. Empowerment strategies are a key to success, although these can add to the problems if discretion is restricted to very operational issues or rendered meaningless by controls and procedures. Empowerment, too, must be related to competence. It can be more stressful for staff to be empowered to act without having the knowledge and skills to act effectively.

So, if empowerment strategies are to succeed, areas of genuine discretion within the structure of jobs first need to be identified. Reviewing accountabilities has, in my experience, inevitably led to delayering. In Eastern Electricity, for example, 28 grades have been reduced to 10. Secondly, empowerment must be reinforced through training and development at the individual and team level. This brings us to the concept of continuous development and the learning organisation. We must actively and explicitly encourage learning. I have discovered the hard way that individual training and development cannot be imposed, or managed solely from the HR department. Individuals must be encouraged to consciously manage their own learning. They will need help in understanding how they learn as individuals, in identifying the assumptions behind their own thinking, and in distinguishing between operational learning (how) and conceptual learning (why).

Finally, the focus on commitment needs to be addressed through effective communication. Further problems are encountered here. Communications are perceived as too 'top-down' with little management interest in the views of the workforce. Written communication can be out of date; team briefings irrelevant. Yet people express an apparently insatiable desire for more information – but information which is pertinent, timely, concise and objective.

I have thought long and hard about these issues, identifying the following ingredients to success:

- Develop a communications strategy which is well thought through, reinforces desired organisational values and empowers front line management as communicators. Have them shape the content of communication rather than writing it and passing it on. This requires front line managers to have a greater level of business awareness than is often the case.
- Develop interactive mechanisms: multi-disciplinary project teams, focus groups, 'speak-up' lunches, staff briefings, review teams and other such forums.
- Monitor progress through regular surveys. To me, the necessary actions in this area have been summed up by John Kotter:

> Communicate the direction as often as possible (repetition is important) to all those people . . . whose help or co-operation is needed; doing so, whenever possible, with simple images or symbols or metaphors that communicate powerfully without clogging already over-used communication channels and without requiring a lot of scarce management time; making the message credible by using communicators with good trade records and working relationships, by stating the message in as sensible a way as possible, by making sure the words and deeds of the communication are consistent, and generally by demonstrating an unswerving dedication to the vision and strategies (so-called 'leadership by example').[5]

Decisions: difficult and otherwise

As all good HR Managers know, we do not have 'difficult' decisions, only decisions with varying degrees of challenge! Many topics spring to mind that cry out for inclusion in this context: refocusing the HR department in Eastern Electricity to remove overlaps and ambiguities; dealing with the personnel implications of introducing cross-functional process teams; deciding on the optimum parameters for a long-term incentive scheme for senior managers.

Inevitably, the most challenging issues arise from the management of change. One example will suffice. The electricity supply industry has, until 1992, managed pay through national-level bargaining on basic pay and essentially automatic progression through salary scales using fixed incremental points. Such a scheme has the benefit of consistency and is, not unexpectedly, strongly favoured by trade unions. However, it has many disadvantages. High achievers do not feel they are differentially rewarded in relation to their contribution. Low achievers do not receive the message through the pay mechanism that this performance level is not acceptable. Pay cannot be used as a driver towards goal attainment.

The difficulty arises in introducing performance-related pay with managers who have little or no experience of making individual judgements on performance, where objectives may not be well defined and where trade union resistance is to be expected. The problems that can arise are:

- A perception that managers' judgements are too subjective, leading to dissatisfaction and a feeling that performance-related pay is divisive and unfair;
- A feeling that performance-related pay is really another form of cost-reduction strategy, since public progression for all is replaced by confidential and variable progression for some;
- Worries that position in the scale will penalise progression, leading to demotivation of potentially high performers nearing their scale maximum;
- A feeling that the emphasis on individual results will detract from team achievement – indeed, may result in too competitive a response from individuals aware of the fact that payments may arise from a fixed pre-defined kitty.

Such problems must be addressed in detail. Most HR

Managers see relating rewards to an individual's contribution as central to improving business effectiveness in the 1990s. Many of the above problems can be alleviated by the timing of the introduction of performance-related pay. Managers will need time to be thoroughly trained in setting objectives and appraising performance, and much individual and team counselling will be necessary in this area – a key role for the HR Manager. In addition, the link between individual performance and team performance needs to be clearly understood. Group incentive plans will continue to be necessary to support specific business strategies, for example by linking pay to units produced, customer satisfaction indices, levels of scrap etc. We need a diversity of reward strategies to suit different circumstances. Within individual performance-related pay, specific objectives can emphasise team goals – and individuals can be rewarded for team performance within the performance-related pay system. Quality objectives, too, can be set within an individual performance management context, ensuring that performance-related pay is consistent with quality initiatives.

Underlying such implementation issues are questions of culture change. If pay processes reinforce the notion of entitlement irrespective of contribution, of tenure irrespective of skill level, then the message is that achievement is less important than service. Most HR Managers will find these to be unhelpful messages in the competitive climate of the mid-1990s. Instead, the emphasis should be on results, on recognition of contributions to objectives, on innovation, on personal accountability . . . and pay strategies need to reinforce these elements of the HR vision.

Competencies

What are we looking for in the people we employ? Much use has been made of competencies in this context – and much money has been paid to consultants investigating this subject.

The advantages of analysing the required competencies in detail are that this can focus on future business requirements for skills and knowledge – and any gap between these future requirements and current capabilities can be identified. This is vital. However competencies can quickly become out of date and often become too general to be meaningful. Also, in defining core competencies, specific technical skills can be underplayed even though these may be vital for job effectiveness.

Within Eastern Electricity, my personal focus has been on senior managers, and the core competencies identified are reproduced in Table 2.

These competencies reflect issues that are valuable in the changing culture of my organisation – particularly the emphasis on strategic vision, action centredness and profit/cost consciousness. Other organisations newly emerging from the public sector will also find relevance here.

For staff generally, a number of common themes emerge, including:

- A strong customer orientation at all times;
- A willingness to improve continuously;
- Being a team player;
- A willingness to take personal responsibility;
- A flexible, adaptable approach;
- An open style.

HR role in the boardroom

I am saddened that only a minority of Heads of HR sit on the main board of their organisation. I believe the presence of the HR Director on the main board to be vital to the effectiveness of the organisation overall, as well as of the HR function. Why? There are at least four reasons:

- The HR presence demonstrates publicly and clearly the

Table 2

Senior Management Core Competencies in Eastern Electricity
(extract)

1. Strategic Change
   - Establishes a course of action to achieve new or changed long-term goals
   - Contributes to development of overall business strategies

2. Leadership
   - Inspires and guides individuals and groups (subordinates, peers and superiors) towards goal achievement.
   - Is proactive and takes charge when required.

3. Teamwork
   - Participates in and facilitates team effectiveness
   - Works effectively with others at all levels to achieve business goals

4. Empowerment
   - Allows others the opportunity to take responsibility and a sense of ownership in jobs or projects without losing overall direction.

5. Breadth
   - Is aware to a high level of the overall business goals
   - Knows the major activities of other Functions

6. Judgement
   - Makes sound and timely decisions which fit the business and the Function concerned.
   - Is able to prioritise well

7. Action-centredness
   - Makes things happen
   - Achieves results – despite the difficulties

8. Quality
   - Is very focused on quality
   - Inspires in others an obsession with continuous improvement and serving the customer

9. Profit/Cost Consciousness
   - Has a thorough understanding of cost and profit drivers in Eastern Electricity
   - Strives to improve cost effectiveness

10. People Management
    - Develops staff effectively
    - Communicates well and listens to others

importance attached to HR management by the organisation. It signals the need, at the highest level, to think
through HR issues alongside financial, marketing and
technical concerns. HR is clearly seen as a business
partner.

- It enables the HR contribution to be made proactively,
both at a strategic level and at the formulating stages of
policy. Resourcing issues, possible IR tensions, succession
questions, communications initiatives and many other
items can be considered whilst the business strategies are
being formulated. This can avoid later problems emerging,
perhaps too late to revise an agreed policy direction.

- HR strategies can be much more soundly based on business
goals if the HR Manager is involved in the business
discussion. However effective the subsequent communication, nothing can substitute for involvement. Even the
best communication after the event will miss the subtle
nuances, the tone, the colour which are so crucial to
understanding the political context within which policies
unfold.

- The HR Manager is a key counsellor and 'sounding board'
for the Chief Executive, bringing objectivity and empathy
to difficult and complex issues facing the CEO and other
directors. Only if the HR Manager is fully aware of all the
interdependencies, pressures, and boardroom priorities,
can this counselling role be fully satisfied.

Against the background of these advantages – the credibility of
the function, the ability to be proactive in policy, the clearer
link between HR goals and business goals, and the ability of
the HR Manager to act as an effective sounding board, why
then are there not more Heads of HR on the main Board!
Sadly, this relates again to a perception of the HR function as
too operational or too intent on social engineering. More
philosophically, others may argue that HR is the responsibility
of senior line directors and they do not need or want a
specialist presence.

Yet, the HR field is an increasingly complex one. Incentive schemes, legal questions, psychometric analyses, demographic trends . . . these issues all require specialist support. In addition to this, however, are the various judgements to be made – about the timing and pace of change, about embedding initiatives, about tracking staff reactions and morale, and individual and team performance, about organisational change. The Head of HR in partnership with the CEO and other directors can add value to these difficult and sensitive areas for the exercise of judgement.

The future, and beyond

The HR vision described in the earlier part of this chapter (see Table 1) proposed a number of likely components of HR in the future: the 'network organisation', a continuing emphasis on empowerment, and the still-developing impact of IT. Tom Peters in *Liberation Management* identifies 27 propositions for the organisation of the future.[6] Included in this list are the following:

- Most value added from products or services of any sort will come from headwork/knowledge work;
- 'Horizontal' business processes, which weld former functional activities into 'seamless wholes', will be the main basis for doing business, and adding value;
- Most of tomorrow's work will be undertaken in project teams;
- There will be constant reorganisation and reporting lines will often change;
- Peer evaluation will be as important or more important than boss evaluation;

Tom Peters strongly emphasises the 'network organisation' concept, which he defines as 'utilising temporary collections of

contractors from all over to accomplish specified tasks'.[7] In his
future scheme of things, there are almost no middle managers.
As a result of IT, access to information will be instant at all
levels of the organisation.

Many other writers are following similar themes. Alvin
Toffler in *Power Shift* sees the 'blistering pace of innovation'
particularly in IT as key to future developments. For him,
there will also be a savage reduction in the number of middle
managers. He says that:

> . . . independent family-run units are once more multiply-
> ing. But in addition we have witnessed the spread of
> franchising which links mom-and-pop operators to the
> financial and promotional clout of large firms. The next
> logical step will come when family enterprises crop up as
> respected, powerful units within large corporations as
> well.[8]

Peter Drucker develops this theme in his *Post Capitalist
Society*. He says for example that large businesses 'require
systematic contracting out of service work to organisations
whose business it is to do such work'.[9]

All these writers may be wrong, but they will at least be
consistently wrong! Those middle managers who are reading
this survey and wondering what they will do can take some
comfort (not much) from Charles Handy who, whilst identifying 'fewer mammoth bureaucracies', more federal organisations and more tiny businesses', also sees 'more requirements
for specialists and professionals in organisations'. He then
asks: how will they be trained and retrained? We may be able
to answer this question. This next question is more worrying:
'What will the rest of us do?'[10]

The HR Manager contemplating the future can discern a
number of trends which will need careful handling. They
include managing:

- The affiliated organisation;
- The lean organisation;

- The empowered organisation;
- The changing organisation;
- The ethical organisation.

Each will be briefly examined in turn.

The affiliated organisation

Given the physical meaning, in my company, of the 'network', I prefer the 'affiliated organisation' as a label to capture the trend towards contracting out. I believe organisations will increasingly ask: what are our core skills? Can some one else do particular tasks better than us? Better here will mean more efficiently, and cheaper. This trend has already embraced catering, security and transport: it will spread to parts of the business hitherto seen as core. Linked to this development will be the increasing trend towards homeworking. I wrote, in 1985, about the challenge of homeworking, including the change of work style for the employee and the manager, and of the importance of setting clear measurable objectives.[11] These issues are still on the agenda in the mid-1990s.

The HR Manager and senior line managers will need to work out the contractual relationships for franchising, home-working and subcontracting, to ensure that performance management disciplines are in place, to work out the communication needs of the contract staff in relation to the core business, to manage boundaries so that the 'disaggregated business' does not become the dysfunctional business, and to manage new learning challenges especially in the IT field. The challenges here are enormous.

The lean organisation

Continuing job losses amongst middle management as organisations delayer will be accompanied by continuing reviews of headcount costs and operational costs at all levels. As the authors of *The Machine that Changed the World* put it:

> The lean producer . . . combines the advantages of craft and mass production whilst avoiding the high cost of the former and the rigidity of the latter. Towards this end, lean producers employ teams of multi-skilled workers at all levels of the organisation and use highly flexible, increasingly automated machines to produce volumes of products in enormous variety. Lean production . . . is 'lean' because it uses less of everything compared with mass production – half the human effort in the factory, half the manufacturing space, half the investment in tools, half the engineering effort to develop a new product in half the time.[12]

HR Managers will continually need to develop effective exit strategies which couple (hopefully) a voluntary approach with reasonable packages and outplacement/counselling services. This latter aspect will become more important, and carry on after employees have left the organisation. Alongside a continuing focus on reduced cost will be maintaining the morale of the core workforce remaining. Management will need to continually seek a climate of understanding about the necessity for organisational changes, and continually improve the capabilities of the core workforce. Reward and recognition strategies will remain vital, with the emphasis changing to group schemes rewarding key parameters including customer satisfaction and profit.

The empowered organisation

As the authors of *Empowering Innovative People* put it:

> . . . companies that are locked into specific management, production or marketing patterns will find themselves outmanoeuvred by those that are ready, willing and able to adjust at all levels. This kind of adjustment will require the use of creative innovators at every level . . .[13]

For the HR Manager, this will continue to involve recognising innovative individuals and providing the climate within which innovation is encouraged.

Linked closely to notions of empowerment is the concept of the learning organisation. Here the focus is on a pervasive learning atmosphere, on continuous improvement, on an openness to knowledge from outside the organisation and on widespread opportunities at all levels for training and development. Self-development will be emphasised, and the coaching and counselling role of team leaders will be a strong feature of the empowered organisation.

The changing organisation

The above themes – affiliation, leanness, empowerment – all involve change. So why a separate category? I believe that the changes over the next 5–10 years will be fundamental – and IT driven. The process re-engineering likely in all organisations will demand special attention to the management of change itself. If we are heading towards what Tom Peters has described as the 'age of unstructure',[14] we need to develop staff willing and able to embrace change, to be at ease with ambiguity.

This challenge for the HR Manager is particularly relevant in newly privatised businesses in the UK such as electricity, water, gas and telecoms. Here the previously public sector culture of stability, of rules, of tenure give way very quickly to cost pressures, IT changes, raised customer expectations and managing regulatory frameworks. Here, and elsewhere, communications will be an important agenda item. As Rosabeth Moss Kanter has put it:

> Too often 'communication' translates into a unilateral directive. Real communication requires a dialogue among the different change makers – a give and take that allows these different 'voices' to express themselves and be listened to'.[15]

In the mid-1990s, the HR Manager will need clear communication strategies which are genuinely two-way, and which embrace the workforces on the contract side of the business.

The ethical organisation

The issue of ethics will become increasingly important to UK businesses as the 1990s unfold. I see two aspects to ethics in organisations. Firstly, the organisational ethical issues. The key question is: what is ethically correct? Ethical issues underpin decisions in many areas including product development, marketing, the environment, financing, reward structures and sales. Press coverage of insider dealing and high-profile legal cases and scandals have raised ethics up the agenda. Unethical behaviour verging on illegality, which leads to adverse PR or, worse, warnings, recalls or monetary penalties, clearly has a major 'bottom-line' implication too. Dealing with ethical issues essentially involves consideration of what is fair with decisions taken on the basis of reasoned judgement rather than pressure, favouritism, or rewards.

For the HR Manager, there are major training issues here, using case studies to sharply illuminate ethical issues. In addition, there is a key link to vision and values since the organisational values should reflect their ethical concerns. Pay for performance, incentive schemes and other reward mechanisms will need to be reviewed from an ethical standpoint.

Secondly, there are individual ethical issues involving questions of privacy, disclosure and personal behaviour. Stephen Covey in the *Seven Habits of Highly Effective People* suggests that each of us needs to think through a personal mission statement – to think through our personal priorities and to align our behaviour with our beliefs. (A freephone USA number is even provided to those of us needing help in developing our personal mission.)[16] Covey describes the 'four dimensions of reward': physical, mental, social/emotional and spiritual. For some, this spiritual component may be merely quaint; for others the emphasis on self-awareness, on conscience and on personal integrity will be a key theme in the late 20th century.

Summary

This chapter concentrated on some of the issues HR Managers will need to grapple with in future years. These are not easy subjects. Managing reductions in headcount, the transition to an 'affiliated' organisation and the sheer pace of organisational change is daunting. In such circumstances it is far better, as I have indicated, to have the HR presence on the controlling board of the organisation. This gives the HR Manager an opportunity to shape the organisation, and the function, in recognition of the issues described in this chapter, and this book.

With or without board membership, the power of vision is the power which derives from thinking clearly about the future, of developing goals, milestones and measures and of sharing such concepts with everyone. Team understanding of shared goals can underpin the successful management of change. The HR Manager, by an involvement in so many of the subjects relevant to an organisation's success, can play a pivotal role in guiding the organisation through the challenges of the 1990s, and beyond. One final word: be proactive!

References

1 See the analysis in Karen LEGGE, *Power, Innovation and Problem Solving in Personnel Management*, McGraw-Hill, London, 1978.
2 For more details see Stephen CONNOCK, *HR Vision: Managing a Quality Workforce*, IPM, London, 1991. Especially Chapters 2 and 3.

3 I have written elsewhere on what makes for a big idea. See Stephen CONNOCK, 'The importance of big ideas to HR Managers', *Personnel Management*, June 1992, p. 24–27.

4 Rosabeth MOSS KANTOR, 'Managing the Human Side of Change', *Management Review*, April 1985, p. 55.

5 John P. KOTTER, *A Force for Change: How Leadership Differs from Management*. Collier-Macmillan, London, 1990, p. 51.

6 Tom PETERS, *Liberation Management*, Macmillan, London, 1992, p. 153–156.

7 ibid p. 122.

8 Alvin TOFFLER, *Power Shift: Knowledge, wealth and violence at the edge of the 21st Century*, Bantam Books, New York, 1990, p. 187.

9 Peter DRUCKER, *Post Capitalist Society*, Butterworth-Heinemann Oxford, 1993, p. 85

10 Charles HANDY, *The Future of Work*, Basil Blackwell, Oxford, 1985, p. 10.

11 Chris BREWSTER and Stephen CONNOCK, *Industrial Relations – Cost Effective Strategies*, Hutchinson, London, 1985, p. 111–114.

12 James P. WOMACK, David T. JONES and Daniel ROOS, *The Machine that Changed the World*, Macmillan, New York, 1990, p. 13.

13 Karl F. GRETZ and Steven R. DROZDIEK, *Empowering Innovative People*, Probus, Chicago, 1992, p. 3–4.

14 Tom PETERS, *op. cit.*, p. 145.

15 Rosabeth MOSS KANTOR, Barry A. SKEIN and Todd D. JICK, *The Challenge of Organisational Change*, Macmillan, New York, 1992, p. 388.

16 Stephen R. COVEY, *The Seven Habits of Highly Effective People*, Simon & Schuster, New York, 1985.

DEVELOPING STRATEGIES

Other titles in this series

HR Effectiveness
Jim Matthewman

Personnel professionals *know* they contribute to business success; all too often, their main task is to get hard evidence to convince others . . .

Internal customers rightly require the same standards of service as those in the marketplace. HR departments can meet their needs – and get thanked for it – only when they start to listen to feedback, commit themselves to quality and continuous improvement, and constantly audit their own performance. Jim Matthewman draws on the experiences of organisations like Glaxo and ICL, KLM Airlines and Bull Information Systems, to provide strategies for HR effectiveness and tools to quantify the results. (What cannot be measured cannot be managed nor communicated to sceptical colleagues.) For all personnel practitioners who feel beleaguered, his book offers both relief and invaluable guidance.

ISBN 0 85292 535 2

Changing Culture: New organisational approaches
Allan Williams, Paul Dobson and Mike Walters

Second edition

'One of the most useful recent works on corporate culture . . . a good starting point for any manager' *Long Range Planning*

First published in 1989, this invaluable book draws on wide-ranging research and the experiences of companies like Abbey National, BP Chemicals and Rank Xerox to reveal how culture change can help drive through significant improvements in performance, efficiency and profitability. Strategic thinking is vital, but the core personnel skills – appraisal, communication, remuneration and training – also play a key role in supporting (or undermining) the process. This major new edition explains just why culture remains crucial and includes stimulating, up-to-date case studies from:

The Royal Mail, McVitie's and James Cropper plc.

Today, all companies faced with fierce competition or declining profits need to look again at their culture in the light of broader change programmes; this clear and accessible text provides precisely the in-depth analysis and guidance they will require.

ISBN 0 85292 533 6

The Institute of Personnel Management is one of the leading publishers of books for personnel professionals, general managers and students. For further information on the full range of IPM titles please contact

The Publications Department
The Institute of Personnel Management
IPM House
Camp Road
London SW19 4UX
Tel: (081) 946 9100